LIVE
UNTIL YOU
DIE

TRAFFORD
PUBLISHING

Note for Librarians: A cataloguing record for this book is available from Library and Archives Canada at www.collectionscanada.ca/amicus/index-e.html
ISBN 1-4120-8284-6

Printed in Victoria, BC, Canada. Printed on paper with minimum 30% recycled fibre. Trafford's print shop runs on "green energy" from solar, wind and other environmentally-friendly power sources.

TRAFFORD
PUBLISHING™
Offices in Canada, USA, Ireland and UK

Book sales for North America and international:
Trafford Publishing, 6E–2333 Government St.,
Victoria, BC V8T 4P4 CANADA
phone 250 383 6864 (toll-free 1 888 232 4444)
fax 250 383 6804; email to orders@trafford.com
Book sales in Europe:
Trafford Publishing (UK) Limited, 9 Park End Street, 2nd Floor
Oxford, UK OX1 1HH UNITED KINGDOM
phone 44 (0)1865 722 113 (local rate 0845 230 9601)
facsimile 44 (0)1865 722 868; info.uk@trafford.com
Order online at:
trafford.com/06-0038

10 9 8 7 6 5 4 3 2 1

About the Author

Reluctant at first to tell her story, Helen Daniel finally agreed to do so when it became clear to her that she might assist others to feel a new sense of possibility through its' telling.

Live Until You Die is the result. It showcases not only Helen's passion for life in all its gutsy glory but also her outrageously wicked sense of humour.

From her violent childhood through the aftermath of her sisters murder, the trauma of a head injury, the wisdom received from her mentors, her journey to Love, and her role as a mother, a grandmother and a foster nan to a teenage Aboriginal boy, Helen's raw and honest sharing of her life opens a door for each of us to walk through.

Contents

THROUGHOUT THE PAGES OF THIS BOOK, you will come across an image of a daffodil in different places.

I have inserted the image amongst the text to prompt you to take a moment and really 'feel' for yourself what you are feeling. There may be new concepts for you to look at. The daffodil is a reminder to take some time to discover how they sit with you. Perhaps go outside for a breath of fresh air, say 'hello' to a bird or simply pause and experience your own energy in that moment.

Preamble

It's taken me many years to write this book. My dedicated team has been hounding me to write my story. My resistance has simply been that I see my life as an ordinary one – no better or worse than anyone else's.

At fifty-two years of age, I am often told that I live an extraordinary life. Yes it's true I've had to deal with what the world would see as incredibly tragic events. But there has been so much more. I have made wonderful connections with Aboriginal people in the Outback with whom I have lived and worked and from whom I have learned lifelong lessons. During the course of my work with the terminally ill, I have made connections with people in their last days of life on this earth that were so real, so full of love and joy, I feel like the luckiest person alive. I have worked in the prison system with people in desperate circumstances where their backs were against the wall. From that place, these men opened to parts of themselves that had been denied them their whole lives. They allowed me to witness those parts, for which I am truly humbled.

In my life today I head up an international company I established to deliver the work I am so passionate about to the world and I have an amazing team of seventeen dedicated people who assist me in doing that. I am driven to take the stories that have been my life and learn from them, take responsibility for them, and work with the lessons to teach others how to do the same. I am passionate about sharing the joy of being connected to the most powerful force on the planet – Nature. It underpins all of the work we do. I learned early in life that we humans take far more from Nature than we give. If we don't turn that around now, we will suffer the consequences.

The other part of my life is as a proud mother of three beautiful, strong capable human beings, and as a grandmother to four precious babies who light my life daily. I am blessed to be a 'foster nan' to an amazing young Aboriginal boy who is fulfilling a life-long dream of playing high level football here in Victoria, Australia. I have an amazing garden that I love to spend time in, and a wonderful loyal dog called Lily, who is my friend and companion.

I have studied lots in my life, while bringing up my kids, and working in a welfare job to keep the wolves from the door.

My life has been full of 'stories' like everyone else's. What drives me today, in my work and in the world, is that people *live* their 'stories' rather than *experiencing* them. People aren't taking the lessons and moving forward. Learning and growing from all that happens. Taking responsibility for what they create.

My work involves 'getting under' the stories that so many people tell themselves, and others, to stay 'safe'. Getting down and dirty, to the truth underneath the many illusions it feels to me that the world lives in.

There is more. There is a journey from the head and all the knowledge and intellect that seems to run the world these days, to the heart. To the truth of who you are. To your Soul. To learning to open up and share yourself and your truth with others.

We are so bound by the rules that society, our families, and others inflict upon us, that we have lost the art of spontaneous communication. Real, gutsy communication. Everything we've done so far has got us to here, but now it's time to do it differently.

From tragedy, I've learned courage, strength and compassion; and from triumph, I've learned humility. In my experience, from triumph most people go to ego. Choosing humility makes it a whole different journey. There *is* a different way to live your lives. There really is.

Looking around the world, I see how we as human beings treat each other – how we don't connect from a deep and true place. There is a deep place of Knowing inside every human being that is sure, safe and unshakable. This place is challenged by almost everything in our lives. It is the toughest place to get to. However, once there, depression, uncertainty and indecision cannot exist. This is the place where real Love exists. Tough, gutsy Love for yourself and others, that leaves you with a strength and courage that nothing can rock. Nothing.

1

Jo's Death

THE DAY BEGAN AS ANY OTHER. NIKI, MY DAUGHTER, WAS home from school with back pain and we were heading to the physiotherapist later that day. The memory of the next hour is crystal clear.

HALFWAY THROUGH THE VACUUMING, THE PHONE rang. It was Mum's neighbour. She sounded hysterical as she told me she could hear Mum screaming.

I ran to the car to make the one-minute drive round there. Niki jumped in with me and we headed out of the driveway.

As we backed onto the road we saw *him* running across the schoolyard opposite our home. He was screaming to us.

"Jo's dead!"

At this point I don't believe my mind registered anything other than 'Just get there'. In that moment, it didn't allow me to take on board what he was actually saying.

He jumped into the car and I drove round the corner to Mum's. The scene will be etched in my memory forever. My mother was on her knees on the front doorstep, sobbing into her hands. I ran to her and lifted her up to look into my face. That look is one that still, even now as I write this, brings an indescribable chill to my blood. She looked into my eyes and cried out with a blood-curdling sound, "She's dead!"

My mind was whirling around. Somewhere inside I believed they had both gone crazy. In a matter of seconds, I told myself over and over again that they had made it up for some sick reason, or that perhaps they had, in fact, gone crazy!

I ran to Jo's room. I stood over her bed, pleading with her to move, begging from some deep place inside, for my beloved baby sister to move and tell me this wasn't happening. Her battered body could not move. It was like some horror movie that was playing out on a screen in front of my eyes.

Still trying to grapple with reality, I ran screaming to the neighbour to come. Somewhere in my mind
I remembered that she was a nurse. *"That's it! She can
fix this! That's logical."* I dragged her physically into Jo's
room and screamed, "Help her, will you!" This poor
woman was actually a child-care nurse and resisted
me all the way to that room. But she had no chance of
fighting the frenzy I was in to prove my sister was still
alive. She was literally dragged there to that bedside,
kicking and screaming, where on looking at Jo's body,
she fell to the ground and sobbed.

Reality started to seep in. She was dead. My best
friend, my baby sister. The one person I trusted in this
entire world was gone. I ran outside and looked to the
sky. *"Why, why why??? Why did you take her away? What has
she done? Who has done this terrible thing to her?"*

My mind was spinning. I was looking into the
faces of onlookers, trying desperately to see something
that looked like sanity; looking for someone who was
going to stand up and say, "It's all been a dream."

All the while *he* was hovering in the background,
crying, trying to cuddle me, asking me to console him.
My mind was in complete turmoil. The next moments
turned this incredibly painful tragedy into another
kind of nightmare. I watched my fourteen-year-old
daughter, who had also just lost the most treasured

aunty and friend she had in the world, circling the periphery of the scene. She looked wary somehow... wary of *him*... as he tried to stay close to us all. She looked at him with disgust and fury. I tried to reach out to her in her pain but she pulled away and stayed in her own space, just watching... and waiting. My mind was in such a confused state, with questions whirring around my brain, along with enormous fear and panic, and all the other things that go along with this level of chaos.

My two brothers, and Peter (Jo's ex-partner and the father of her children), had arrived from somewhere. It seemed like the next moment we were surrounded by police cars, police armed with guns, television news units and trucks with huge cranes on the back with men filming our every move. Police had grabbed *him* and were holding him against my car. He was pleading with me to explain how he loved her.

All of a sudden, a feeling I have never before experienced started to creep into my body. It felt like ice water being poured into my veins from the toes upward.

The penny dropped. The reason my daughter wouldn't come near him was that she knew. Inherently. He had killed my sister. *"Oh my God, noooooooooooooooooo!"* He had come to my house last night, shaking and sick, sallow skin and frightened eyes. He told me that Jo had fought with him and how upset he was.

"Oh Christ, don't tell me I had comforted my sister's murderer?"

The night before began to unfold for me as yet another horrendous nightmare. He had come to our door asking for help, telling us about the fight they'd had, asking us to drive him home, which my partner did… all this to cover his tracks, using *me* to cover his tracks. He told us that the police had been called as he and Jo had been shouting. He went out and spoke to the police and they left. *"Oh my God, it's all falling into place. The police left. My sister was in there beaten to a pulp and they left because he told them it was okay. Why didn't they insist on seeing her? Why did they walk away? Could they have saved her?"*

We would never know. Neither would the young constable who came to us days later to ask for forgiveness – to own his part in this movie that was playing out. It was beginning to feel like I was never going to cope with what was in front of me. I looked at the sky again, begging Jo to be there for me, with me.

How could she be? It was all closing in on me. I can remember throwing up in the gutter outside the room where my sister lay; I remember looking around at the TV cameras, at all the prying eyes of the neighbours. Then someone said "What about the kids?" I knew in that second that I had to pull myself together – somehow. God only knew how, at that moment, but I had to do something.

I went into auto-pilot and called the school. I knew the headmaster well. I told Bob what had happened and asked him to keep the kids there until I called to say the police and cameras had gone. There was something in having to do this that took me somewhere outside myself for a short while. It all became quite surreal.

As the children (my other two, and Jo's two babies, Matthew and Kate) were led down the street after school by the headmaster, another level of reality hit me. I had to tell these babies their mother was dead. *"How the hell do I do that? Where do we start?"*

Each child reacted in a different way. The terror and pain that followed for these children cannot be described on paper. Jo's children were nine and six at the time of her death. Their journey without their mother, and the trauma of the court cases that followed, are a whole other story that needs to be told at some point.

That night, as we sat around the lounge room together trying to make sense of what life looked like now, trying to understand, from the corner of the room where the TV was playing the latest news; I saw something that shocked me to my core.

As I watched the screen, my mother's house came into view – there it was in full colour. I watched in silence as the funeral men carried my baby sister out of the house in a body bag. I passed out. When I opened my eyes I knew my life would never be the same. In that moment I needed to make a choice. Somehow, I had to fight against going under myself. I needed to hold this family together. Somehow, in that very moment, I made a choice to fight.

Fight for my own life. For the lives of my children. For the lives of Jo's children. Also, for my poor grieving mother who was trying desperately to come to grips with finding her daughter dead in her bed.

It was there, amongst the ashes, the black feelings of hopelessness, and my utter despair and grief, that I found that unique place that was the strength of who I truly am. That place in me that I had to draw on to rise up like the phoenix and do whatever it was going to take to turn our lives around, and to give these children the best life I could possibly give them, with the love I had inside.

2

The Knowing

LEADING UP TO THE DAY OF JO'S DEATH, THERE WERE MANY signs along the way. The deep Knowing inside each one of us is protected or denied at different levels throughout our lives, depending on the level of trauma involved, or the amount of effort it would take in our lives to accept the Knowing and change the life accordingly.

Some choose to ignore the Knowing completely and live life as directed by others. Society, family, partners, children, the media, the boss, friends, the church ... really anyone outside of themselves who will make a decision so they don't have to. This choice is common and comes from not wanting to take personal responsibility for what we create in our own lives.

It has always been my belief that we create our own reality. Now was the time to learn that at a much deeper level. It's easy to say those words as a belief. Now I had to really dig deep to hold for that.

The day before Jo's death, our dear friend Lionel Rose and I tried desperately to talk her into flying interstate to escape the failing, and quite aggressive, relationship she was in. We offered to pay her airfare and send her to stay with friends.

Something in both Lionel and I knew that clearly, things were not right. As we looked at her across the table, there was a look that I recognise now as one of determination to stay. Who knows why? We'll never know what Jo's inner Knowing was telling her that day.

On the day of her death, Jo spent the day with Mum after weeks of bickering. They enjoyed each others company. Jo spoke of being so relieved to be home. Mum went out, bought Jo's favourite food and cooked a meal, which they shared together with Kate, Jo's six-year-old daughter.

As Mum left for work that night, an impulse told her to take young Kate to a friend of hers to spend the night to allow Jo a good night's sleep. This deep inner Knowing in my mother, to share this gorgeous meal together, then to take Katie from the house and place her somewhere safe, never came through as a rational thought – just a Knowing, deep inside, that something was about to unfold.

That same night, as the tragedy did unfold, Mum's neighbour was trying to call my home to tell me about the fight that was raging next door with Jo and this man, but my daughter Niki was on the phone to a friend, and the neighbour could not get through.

Niki felt enormous guilt for a long time afterwards for being on that phone. The fact is, she was, and what Knowing was she following? If the neighbour had reached us, I would have gone to the aid of my sister.

Today, my own Knowing tells me that, if I had been called and gone to the house, I could also have been killed. That was not my journey. My part in this was to be there for the children.

The next morning, he had come running across the schoolyard screaming at me that Jo was dead. Niki was with me. We went to the house, and all the while Niki knew inside her heart that he had killed our beautiful Jo.

The law states that if police are called to a domestic dispute, they have to sight both parties. The two young constables who went to the house that night were persuaded by this man that Jo was okay, and they didn't insist on seeing her. They took his word and left. Whether or not they could have saved her life, whether or not she was alive at that moment, the fact remains that it didn't happen. As a family, being confronted by this young policeman in tears, two days after her death, something in us that knew he had played his part too. No blame, no anger. It wasn't about forgiving anyone, really. This was just a deep feeling inside all of us that there was no more to be done here.

The grieving process was an unfolding. Mum stayed up all night and read novels. She had moved into a caravan in our back yard with Kate, as going back to her home where Jo was killed was too much for her to bear. Nine-year-old Matthew shared Tim's room. He found it difficult to cope in those early days. He cried and sleep-walked for the first twelve months and, to save our sanity, we had a roster, which included Niki (who was fourteen), Peta (eleven), Tim (nine) and myself.

When we heard the crying, whoever was on roster that night would get up. The first challenge was finding him, as he'd usually be curled up in a corner somewhere calling for his mum. We had a process to keep him safe, as he was normally unaware of what was taking place. We led him gently back to bed, then settled him down by rubbing his back until he was fully asleep once more.

Kate was only six and couldn't comprehend a lot of what was going on, just the feeling of not being able to see her mum again. Her journey has been a challenging one, as a young girl growing up without her mother. My mother, Marg, has been a beacon of light for Kate, now twenty-four, who with her gorgeous partner Ratsy (Mark), still spends a lot of time with Mum.

Matthew's distress became more and more evident as the weeks went on, and he expressed a need to see the type of coffin his mother was buried in. His memory was such that he couldn't remember being at the funeral (only six to eight weeks before). I arranged for the funeral director, Robert, who had been in charge of Jo's funeral, to show us the room where the coffins were kept, to give Matt an idea of how they looked. I passed out on entering the room, which was a great help!

Matt had insisted Tim go with him, so the two nine-year-olds proceeded to inspect the coffins, assisted by Robert. Matt had to see the inside of the coffin to satisfy himself that his mother would be comfortable.

On reflection, it seemed that Matt settled quite

considerably being able to put some part of his mind at rest. Tim, who was as white as a sheet but knew inside he had to help his cousin through this ordeal, went into his own survival mode. He was, even at nine, a keen money saver. He had been saving pocket money since he was four, and started asking how much the coffins would cost and how much they went up in price each year. Who knows where that was going?

Peta had nightmares and was very frightened for a long time. From all of these children in so much grief and fear came a concept that I now use in my practice with many clients. 'Keep the fear at Number 1'. It evolved into a game with the children. As their thoughts ran away with them in the night, or as their fear grew, the game gave them the ability to come back to what was real, the fear itself, and not let them run away with the fantasy. 'Keep it at Number 1; don't allow it to get to 3, or 4, or 24. Always bring it back to Number 1.' It was a simple way of eventually allowing them to feel some peace.

When I received a letter from Peta, who had gone on a school camp full of fear that she wouldn't cope for a week, and on the back of the envelope was: "I'm keeping it at Number 1", I cried with relief.

As the world is so fear-driven these days, people are out of control before they know it. This simple process itself, has helped many people who struggle with that thousand monkey syndrome (the chatter in the head that won't stop) to find some peace.

Niki had been witness to the whole drama unfolding on that day. Her way of coping was to get angry. It was a huge journey for Niki to come through to the other side of that anger. What kept her sane, I believe, is her deep level of love and compassion. Her anger was evident in her behaviour, but her love for her siblings and cousins brought into focus the need for her to love them and help them through as well. Every day, another battle between the head and the heart was being fought.

The following months were filled with taking care of the family. The added pressures of the pending court case, newspaper reports, and men arriving at our door at all hours of the night warning us not to testify against this man, added to the melting pot of emotions that were running through the house. A very colourful character who had known the family for some time, arrived one day and offered to have the man who had committed this horrendous act 'done away with', as he put it.

I have to say right now, that before that day, it would have shocked me to my core. Now, if I'm honest, I did think about it for a few seconds. How easy would that be? 'An eye for an eye.' After all, this was my baby sister. This was something that I, like millions of other people, I'm sure, have said time and again, "If anyone hurts my family, I will kill them". Well, here was my chance. All I had to do was say "Yes".

I guess that now, on reflection eighteen years later, those are the head and heart moments I have learned to trust, that bring me to the present time.

I knew in my gut that it wasn't right. My head fought desperately to convince myself that I should accept. If I didn't, wasn't I letting Jo down in some way? Letting down her children? Still, I knew it wasn't right. I said "No".

I fought with myself a lot in those times. For example, during the court case, just before it was my turn to testify, there was a phone call to say there was a bomb in the courtroom. We were rushed out of the room all together, even the accused, who was dragged past us, inches from our faces. He even turned and spoke to my mother as he passed.

My head said all kinds of violent horrible things. However, the two policemen who ushered him out were holding him by the back of his pants, violently shoving and moving him through the crowd.

Somewhere inside me, there was a place that felt something different. I don't even particularly want to write this here on paper. However, I promised myself when starting this book that it would be an honest account of my life. Without laying bare these struggles between my head and my heart, it would not be honest. It would not give an accurate account of my having been given so many examples of how to choose differently. I felt compassion for a fellow soul being treated like an animal.

My head raged. *"How could I feel that? He killed my sister! He's an animal!"* I can't tell you why I have to own the other feeling. I just do.

Over all of that time, one of the things that my entire family found was that people were uncomfortable around us. There was an awkwardness around even the word 'murder', which obviously struck fear into the hearts of people. I'm not sure why that is, really. It's probably something people don't want to think too much about, for fear of it happening in their own family. Perhaps it's that if it can happen to people you know, it's really close to home and that is too much to bear.

It wasn't only the adults in our family who felt this; the children felt it as well. There are always angels, though. The family next door, who we had known before this just as neighbours, became one of those beacons of light at the end of the tunnel. Cass came to me one afternoon, as I walked up and down the footpath in front of our house. I don't even know why I walking up and down. I guess it was one of those survival-mode things that I did to stop me from thinking. Cass simply said, "You look lost". It was enough to drop me into another place and start to feel again.

Cass, Mick and their children opened their door and their hearts to us in those days, and not only did I find solace in their family, my children found real heart-felt friendships with their kids that still exist today.

Some time after Jo's death, another young girl was murdered in our local area, under gruesome circumstances. Naturally, our hearts went out to her family. In that same week, the girl's mother was interviewed on television. At the time, I remember thinking how brave she was to get up and speak so soon after such a tragedy.

The interview was conducted by Melbourne journalist, Derryn Hinch. Sitting there, listening to that conversation with tears streaming down my face, I realised that my whole family and I were craving real communication.

Derryn conducted this interview in a way I hadn't seen or experienced before. In that space of time he allowed this grieving mother to go through the pain of her ordeal and to speak about it without being shut down. He kept the door open for her to keep going. He didn't ask ridiculous questions that put her on the back foot; he seemed to me to be fearless in that moment of just allowing her to do what she needed to do.

 It was a moving experience for me to see someone keep their own thoughts and opinions out of the way to allow another person the space they need to begin the healing process. Today in the work that I do, that's what I teach. There's such a lack of real honest connection between people.

This is my story, but for every one of us in every moment – workplace, home, family, etc., we are led by others who are making choices for us *simply by having an opinion on our lives*. This makes it almost impossible for us to go to that deep place inside and feel what is right for each of us in that moment. In my experience, most people are not truly 'coming from their own gut'.

What I see in my work now, every single day, is that when people don't make those tough decisions from their own gut, nothing is sustainable in their life.

3

The Flying Fox

IT'S INTERESTING, THAT PLACE BETWEEN ADRENALIN AND complete peace and safety – even if it lasts only for a moment or two.

The arguing would start as a few cross words. Maybe some raised voices. That's when the stomach would go into knots. That glazed-over feeling would creep into us kids at that point. We may look across at each other, but there was no feeling in those looks. It was like "I know what's coming and I'm out of here".

Out of here energetically, I mean. We were too little to run too far away. So we'd zone out. Pretend we were miles from there. When the violence started, there was nowhere to 'zone out' to, and nowhere to run. This was the truth of our existence much of the time.

I remember a night when Peter, my older brother, ran to help our mother. He must have been all of six years old. He confronted my father with all of his six-year-old might. Our father threw my brother so hard, his body broke through the wall. He fell, battered and bruised, to the floor. His imprint was in that wall for a long time.

I tried. I jumped up and lashed out at him. "STOP HURTING HIM! STOP HURTING HER! STOP HURTING US!" I remember that chant well.

I have to point out here that this is not about blame. This is not about saying my life was bad or hard. My life was what it was, and I have deep love for my mother and my siblings. I have learned well from my experiences. My father came to teach us, and for me, in my life, he did that well.

My brother's friend 'Smithy' was sleeping over that night. It was always special when someone slept over. We got to have roast dinner and sweets afterwards. The smells from the kitchen made me feel warm inside. With the fire blazing in the fireplace, life was good.

During dinner, a familiar feeling floated in. There was tension between Mum and Dad and that always made me nervous. I remember thinking, *"No, this won't happen tonight, we've got Smithy here."*

Not long after dinner, we were sent to our rooms. I don't remember a lot about the next hour or so, except that the yelling got louder, and the need I felt to protect Smithy grew. He looked very frightened already and my older brother and I knew there was a lot more to come. As the yelling grew in intensity, he began to tremble. We tried every fun activity we could think of, everything we knew, to avoid what was happening in the kitchen.

Then the thing we dreaded most was happening under our noses. He was hitting her. Mum knew better than to cry out, so the dull sobs were almost inaudible, but you can't hide the sound of Mum hitting the floor time after time. Or her trying to crawl to her room while he stood above her, yelling and beating her.

We knew this was going to get worse. There were those times when we could just zone out. We were masters at shutting down the mind and body and, somehow, in amongst the chaos, just drifting off to sleep. But this time we had Smithy sitting with us, terrified.

We heard him coming down the hallway. We moved quietly and swiftly. Within minutes we had my younger sister and brother (at the time probably aged three and five) out of their beds, and Smithy in tow, running as fast as we could through the hallway, down the back steps and out into the yard. We could see the trees ahead. This was something we did often, but this time we had to take care of Smithy as well as the babies.

In those moments, there are some things that a nine-year-old knows about how to stay safe.

Running towards the towering pine trees in our backyard we somehow know inherently, that if we don't make it up those trees to our flying fox in time, things are getting decidedly worse. That was not an option for us. It didn't matter so much for Peter and myself, really. We were prepared to put ourselves in the firing line. But it really mattered about our younger siblings, and it really mattered about Smithy. We had to do this.

We hit the trees at a very fast pace. Up I went with my baby sister by the hand, dragging her up as fast as I could, my brother behind me, shinnying up that tree like a monkey, dragging my little brother after him. Then back down for Smithy. Begging him to hurry.

No time to think as we shoved each sibling into the small, hand-held wire shopping basket, which was our vehicle to safety on the other side where our cubby hut awaited us. Each one of us, in turn, flying between these two trees to safety as fast as we could go. Finally, when each one of us was tucked up in the cubby house, safe and sound, we turned to Smithy and saw the look of horror on his ten-year-old face.

That night, he had obviously experienced domestic violence for the first time in his life. Had been rushed from a warm house out into the cold winter night, dragged a good fifteen feet up a thirty-foot pine tree, shoved into a wire shopping basket and pushed very fast towards the tree twenty-five feet away. When you hit that tree on the other side, there were no cushioned arrival mats. You hit it and scrambled to the makeshift platform we'd erected to climb to the cubby house.

There was a look that passed between my brother and I that night that had passed between us many times previously, and has many times since. I guess that look really said, *"Doesn't everyone live like this? Don't all kids have to have a safe place to hide when these things happen? After all, in a few hours he'll be asleep and we will be fine again."*

There was a feeling of freedom at the top of those

trees. We found solace in our home above the ground. Nobody could reach us there, and we felt the strength of each other. No words were really spoken at these times. There was an inner Knowing, just like the one we felt when the trouble started. We would feel it end the same way. We knew when it was safe to come down.

It was a wonderful training ground for the work I do now. Following the energy and knowing what the truth is.

4

Survival

LOOKING BACK ON THE CHAPTER ABOUT THE FLYING FOX. I would like to convey that as kids we didn't even register that we were in danger. We were in complete survival-mode and it worked very well. We were intuitive, ingenious and we survived.

That last chapter or any other chapter written in this book is not written from the perspective of us being victims. We weren't victims then and we aren't now. We've told this story for years and laughed about the fact that we had no idea that the situation in the flying fox was a scary one. In fact, each member of my family possesses a strong will, a deep inner Knowing, and most of all, a robust sense of humour.

I learned many things during those times that have given me the strength and the ability to teach people about the truth.

Looking back on our friendship with Smithy and other kids like him, it's clear he was traumatized by what happened, and yet we looked at him and felt sorry for him. We looked at his family and saw a sterile picket fence. A family that looked, to the outside world, to be the perfect family: the mother, father and kids. No one raised a voice, everyone had smiles painted on their faces, and they were churchgoers ... so, the story to us should have been that, with their perfect life, they had it all. But my brother and I knew when we walked into their house, that there was something missing.

Of course that didn't mean the extremes in our life were what was required. It was just something we recognised. Things were tricky at our house, no doubt about that, but somehow it gave us a Knowing about how things worked, and the courage to fight. The thing about what I refer to as Picket Fences is that they create apathy. A feeling of not being able to rock the boat for fear of upsetting someone. Someone was often upset in our house, so it was different.

Millions of kids live with domestic violence and learn to survive. This doesn't serve them in living a whole, fulfilling life for themselves. We learn behaviours to protect ourselves, and shut down our feelings, because to feel what's happening is too scary and too painful. There's a huge gap between the true essence of who we are and the personality that we present to the world. All this has been spoken about many times before, but there's a way we can learn to action. A way to reignite the flame.

Domestic violence is just one of millions of things that snuff out the flame. It's an obvious one, and one I'm familiar with, so it's easy to write about it. There are people out there who have never experienced anything like that, and it's probably a horror story to them, but in their own life, there could be one seemingly tiny incident that occurs, which shuts them down in exactly the same way.

The trouble, then, is that they look at others and say, "I've had it easy compared to them. How can I complain?" or, "What is wrong with me that I can't connect, or love truly and passionately?"

 Snuffing out the flame is snuffing out the flame no matter how it happens.

The pain it causes in living an unfulfilled life, instead of the life you are born to live and that you deserve to live, is the same *no matter what the cause.*

The kind of life I'm talking about here is one where, every day when you wake up, you cannot wait to get out of bed and thank God for your existence. For the lessons and the challenges you receive every day of your life. Whether they are fantastic or not.

A smile from a stranger. An opportunity to serve someone. A chance to go to work and do what you love doing. A chance to find someone today to share a single moment of true connection with. An opportunity to spend time in Nature, receiving the wonderful gifts that it offers. Then the chance to give back, and put some work into helping the planet in return. It's all about giving and receiving. These days, I see so much more taking than giving. It's at such a deep, ingrained level that we've lost sight of what counts.

I believe Smithy's family lived within what I call the Picket Fence syndrome. It's something which is so crippling to our society, yet it's not talked about. Like any horrendous act. Like the way people avoided talking to us after Jo's death. To me it's not much different.

Living within the Picket Fence is everything it sounds like. It's living in denial of your true feelings.

It's living in relationships that don't serve you. It's that glazed-over look that I see on the faces of so many people in the world. The living dead, I call them.

It's living in fear of finding out the truth of what you feel in case it changes something in your life. Changes something that may or may not be working, but the fear is of the change. It's the fear of speaking up, often in case of offending and in case you don't look good. It's the fear of losing control of a situation. So it's better to put up with crap than lose control.

I see many couples in my practice, and am always astounded at how little they communicate the truth to each other. The little secrets kept that build into marriage busters, all because they didn't want to rock the boat.

There are many people who've done lots of work on themselves in this area, and are doing quite well. But when I look around the world, I don't see millions of people living passionate lives. I see a lot of people living half-lives for fear of knocking over the Picket Fence.

And that Picket Fence doesn't only pertain to families or couples. It can be the Picket Fence created by your job. Your parents. Society.

I see lots of self-help gurus in the world today who are making squillions of dollars, and probably loving what they do, but my observation, and I've re-searched this extensively, is that they hold themselves above people to achieve their status. They preach and talk down to people about how they need to live their lives. They show off their luxury lifestyles and, at the end of the day, if the people don't make it, it's because they're not 'ready', or some other excuse, so that the guru stays safe. They have what I call the 'special thing' going on. So, no matter how much money or status they have, if they are not connecting to other human beings from a true and real place, instead of from their egos and ivory towers, they are missing something.

In fact they are missing a lot.

5

The Moving Annexe

SOME OF OUR MOST WONDERFUL TIMES AS KIDS WERE SPENT on the foreshore at Blairgowrie, a beautiful little beachside place on the Mornington Peninsula here in Victoria. We had a permanent camping spot for our caravan, which had a great annexe, and we spent six weeks there every summer, swimming and fishing. Hanging out with our friends and just being kids.

Just thinking about it brings warm memories that I cannot describe. My father always worked through

Christmas, so it was just Mum and us kids. A lot of the time with our maternal grandparents, Nanna Ruby and Pa, too.

It was relaxing and joyful. As we grew to be teenagers, my brother Peter and I were allowed to go out at night and hang out on the beach and the sand dunes with all the other teenagers in the park. We had a ball. I think I kissed my first boy down there behind those sand dunes. I can't remember who he was exactly, but it was a hell of a lot of fun! Outdoor movies played on big screens on the foreshore for the kids at night. It was one big party that lasted for weeks.

Families gathered there every Christmas from all over the place to spend holidays and share time with others. It was like a little community, really. We so looked forward to those times together.

I guess the strongest feeling I got in those times was one of safety. There were no arguments, no fighting at all. It was like heaven on earth. Mum would hold barbeques and socialize with the neighbouring people. It was so good to see her relax and have fun.

Pa would take us to the water each morning to swim. We were fifty feet from the waters edge, and it was amazing to be able to go and have a dip whenever we felt like it. To this day, I have a strong love of the water and swimming. Perhaps that's where it started.

It almost felt like being someone else during these times. Like we were 'another' family. One which was normal, and having a good time, like everyone else. I'm sure a percentage of the families around us had their own 'stuff' going on. It's funny how the world plays the game.

Let me explain something here. It didn't seem like we were lacking in anything. It's funny how we make it look okay. Mum was one of those mum's who are on every committee – a community-minded person, proactive in assisting the community to grow. I imagine these times at Blairgowrie were a godsend for her as well. One sunny, summer afternoon however, things changed for me forever.

My father arrived to spend the weekend with us. I'm sure we all tried to be happy that he was there, and maybe we were for a while. As the afternoon rolled on and he started to notice the obvious friendships Mum had developed with the neighbours, the tension started to build. He was a very jealous man and he didn't like for a minute that Mum was talking to these guys – and women, for that matter.

That night, as we arrived back from our beach walk and climbed into bed in the annexe, it was easy to feel what was going on even if we couldn't hear it. In hindsight, as I sit and type this now, it's absolutely hilarious. The fight got underway and as the voices got a little louder, we put our heads under the blankets to try and block out what was going on.

Within minutes, we were looking up at the stars. My father had got into the car, hooked up the caravan and driven off down the little dirt track that led through the caravan park! The annexe had been pulled up along with the van and was flapping along behind it. We were lying there in our bunks underneath the beautiful night sky.

I can't even remember what happened next. I think he may have come back, set up the camp again and left. Not sure really. All I knew then was that my time in Blairgowrie was changed forever. I felt humiliated that the other kids now knew how we lived. After that, we still went there for Christmas holidays but, for me, it never held the same excitement.

Today I can truly belly laugh about that night. It seemed so dastardly then, but there really was a funny side to it. In fact, I believe I remember us kids laughing, even then, the next day, at what it felt like. If only the other kids hadn't heard what went on!

Domestic violence takes so many shapes and forms, all as damaging as each other. But as I've said many times, my life has been dramatic. I obviously need 'dramatic' to get it. So many millions of people live with milder versions of the same thing, and yet never complain because 'it doesn't seem too bad'.

A client told me the other day about her upbringing, where her middle-class parents gave the kids everything money could buy. They grew up on the 'right side of town'.

Her father spoke over the top of her mother at every opportunity. Her mother's voice was silenced in the name of keeping the peace. Father being the authority in the house meant Mother had to sacrifice her own life, her own Knowing, to avoid rocking the boat. The children had to do the same. "Try to be quiet. Daddy's tired". "Be good. Daddy's got a lot to do".

This woman, now in her mid-forties, learned to put the blanket over her feelings and numb out. To the world this looks okay. She's an intelligent, wealthy woman doing okay. But she has absolutely no passion for life and not much idea how to find it. Her flame has been snuffed out, too. The difference is, perhaps, that the things which snuffed out my flame for a time were dramatic, so I stood up time and again to fight. This woman didn't know where to fight from or what to fight for. She learned to shut down her feelings and go into apathy.

The apathy in the world is astounding. How many times in 'ordinary' people's lives do they feel unsafe and allow whatever it is to continue because 'it's not too bad'? How often do they shut down their feelings and put up with dominance and fear, even mild versions? This issue affects our society in such a huge way. Again, it is about snuffing out the flame of who we truly are. Making us second guess ourselves. How can we stand up when we've been told to put up and shut up? How can we know ourselves fully when everywhere on the planet, people are competing and trying to take each other down – even in small ways – to stay on top and be one better?

It's in every teenager feeling the need to be something other than simply themselves, so that they have a chance of being noticed in this world. It's no wonder to me at all that these kids are turning more and more to drugs and alcohol these days to numb out the constant need to prove themselves to the world.

I was recently speaking to a police officer running a campaign in our area for kids in primary schools, to make them aware of what is going on and assist them with their self-esteem. It sounds like a great program. This young guy was conveying to me his absolute disgust at the drug situation in our area and his passion for doing his best to help.

I applaud him.

6

That 'f' Word

WHAT DOES IT MEAN TO YOU? THAT LITTLE WORD WITH SUCH big connotations?

That word 'forgiveness'?

For a very long time the idea of forgiveness was foreign to me. I understood in my head what people said it meant, but in hindsight, I had no idea how to get there. I had learned many techniques of letting go over the years: writing forgiveness letters; reading book after book about choosing Love; attending lectures about judgement and how being angry at someone only affects yourself. But when it came right down to it, all those things meant zip unless I could feel the true meaning of forgiveness.

My father had been ill for what seemed like a really long time. A heart attack and several strokes had left him in very poor health. My mother had gone to stay with him, to take care of him on his return from hospital. I'd heard about his condition from my family, over and over again, and still had no desire to see him or communicate with him or, in fact, with anyone else about him – much to my family's angst.

I woke from a dream that I cannot remember to this day. Not that it matters. The only thing I do remember is that, on waking, a voice said loud and clear: "Go and see your father".

I challenged this for ten minutes or so, but the voice was insistent and very strong.

"You need to see your father now!" I had many arguments going on inside my head at this point, convincing me I had no desire to see him and, in fact, did not want to see him at all. The 'why should I's?' such as "Why should I go out of my way for him when he treated us the way he did?" However, my energy had me stepping out of bed, putting on my clothes and walking out to the car to begin the two-hour drive to my father's home. Several times on the way, I stopped the car to turn back, and the arguments between my head and my heart raged constantly, until I pulled up outside his modest West Rosebud unit in the early morning.

"*No turning back now, just get in there and get it over with*". My mind was in turmoil. "*What do I say to him? How do I approach this man I'd turned my back on for so long*"? All I knew was, I had to put one foot in front of the other. That's all I knew in that moment.

When I knocked at the front door, my mother greeted me with a look somewhere between relief and fury that it had taken me so long to finally get there. I ignored it and walked through to where my father sat at the kitchen table.

The time between the door and the table could have only been a few moments, but it seemed like hours. As I walked towards him, I took in everything. His furniture... always the same... brown vinyl couches, brown laminated kitchen table with brown vinyl chairs.

Everything felt very familiar, yet somehow so vastly different. It smelled the same ... that vague memory of tingling in my nose that would alert me to my father's presence. Years rolled through my mind. The games people play, to ignore what is going on in one's family, all presented themselves to me in those few steps between the door and the table.

Then he was there. Sitting, leaning on the table in his very familiar position – hands folded together, shoulders leaning forward and head tilted up, looking straight at me. I stopped for a moment to take in the picture. Was this my father? Everything looked the same, everything smelled the same, everything felt so familiar ... except him.

A memory wafted through my mind.

We are eating our dinner ... my father is really angry with me ... he kicks the chair out from under me ... throws me against the wall. I've been really bad. Mum says, "Be good or he'll get mad. Be a good girl".

"I'll try, I'll really try ... No I won't. I hate you all!" I push my plate onto the floor. I look him straight in the eye, daring him to belt me. There is fire in his eyes. He's going to belt me. I brace myself. Clench my teeth. I'm ready ...

The lino is cool on my face ... it's grey ... it's got big squares on it like a huge jigsaw puzzle. A little bit of blood trickles into the puzzle. A big, giant jigsaw puzzle.

I looked back at this shell of a man that was once my powerful, domineering father – looked into the eyes of a frightened old man who had little time left to reconnect with the daughter he'd been asking to see for months.

It's hard to describe what I felt in those first few moments. Pain and sadness? Yes, I guess there was some of that. The astounding thing was that these feelings were not about me, they were about him. My heart went out to him. I don't think I had ever felt such compassion for another human being as I did in that moment.

Don't get me wrong. As I said, I'm not even sure what forgiveness means. My head was also doing that thing again, telling me I should hate him for treating us so badly.

For me, the greatest lesson of all was allowing myself to feel the truth, rather than the illusion of what my mind had convinced me I had to feel. I wanted to be angry with him for the things he did to me as a child. However, what I needed was to *feel* the truth of what I felt with everything else stripped away.

We spoke for a long time about life and regret and the sadness of years lost. We also spoke about the garden he'd created, and about my siblings. About the death of my sister and the meals he liked to eat. He shared with me his great anxiety over the past weeks, and wondered whether I could help him with some of my 'funny' medicine (homeopathics). I agreed that I would do this for him the following day.

There, across the table, I listened to my father for the first time in my life. I heard his stories, and I heard him clearly when he said, "I've missed you." And I be-

lieved him. I didn't respond in kind, as I really don't think I had missed him at all. But I did believe him in that moment.

When I left that afternoon with the promise of returning with something to help his nerves, I knew I would never see him again. I walked out of that door and thanked God for the opportunity to experience my father in a different way. I no longer feared him. I no longer hated him. I no longer had to protect myself from him or anyone else. Somehow, in that incredible day, I had found that "f" word, in all its glory.

I don't believe in forgiveness in the way I hear it described in the world. This was not about me forgiving my father for the violence he bestowed upon me as a child. Violence and abuse are power-based. Therefore, the people on the receiving end of that violence and abuse, most often live their lives searching for power, or abusing others with power, or giving away their power to stay comfortable. I believe that, in that time with my father, I had another look at those things. I started to see them in a different way. That's not to say I got over myself right there and then, but the journey to freedom had begun.

Having done that, I could also release the obvious power that I had held over my father by removing myself from his life – my way of controlling the controller. During that day, my father and I both found freedom. Not forgiveness … freedom.

My father passed away peacefully that night. I have no remorse for the years I chose not to see him. I also had no guilt at all over being at his funeral, at which one particular aunt threw looks of disgust and "How dare you?" at me for most of the day. These things mattered not to me. I had made decisions about how to get through my life, and how to re-connect with my heart and with my feelings, and that was affecting others. So be it.

I decided long ago not to play the game – the game called life that forbids you to make a stand that might put other people into uncomfortable positions. Most people are afraid to look truthfully at, and speak about, abuse and violence issues too loudly in case their own lives are affected. Or in case they have to do something outside of themselves. This blanketing effect cripples our society, not only with abuse and violence, but also with the need to be right – the need to control.

It's not allowing others the freedom to express their own energy in their own way.

7

Learning as we Grow

THERE IS SO MUCH I LEARNED FROM MY FATHER THAT IT'S HARD to know where to begin and end.

Yes, he was a violent man with a vile temper, and he took it out on us. On the other hand, he provided for us extremely well. We were the first kids on the block with a TV in 1957 when they were first introduced to Australia. He drove a big, shiny Mack truck, which I was very proud to sit in and drive up our street. We were the envy of a lot of kids.

As a child, I felt a lot of confusion between my

head and my heart. I wanted to love my father the same way I loved my mum, my maternal grandparents and my siblings. I would look at him sometimes and see such sadness it would affect me deeply. I would see him when we visited his parents. I don't call them my grandparents. I was terrified of them.

They were cold and unfeeling to us. His father would sit at the end of the table, tapping his fingers and just staring at us with a look that made me go cold. Every now and then I would wonder how it must have been for my father, growing up in a house with these people. I wondered how that must have affected the way he parented us.

I don't condone domestic violence in any way. But I learned, somehow, to shut out the feelings enough to survive, and I guess he must have too. Of course, this shutdown is certainly not sustainable or conducive to a healthy life. In fact, years later, I joined a self-help group and it was during my time there that I started to understand that the behaviour my father exhibited wasn't normal.

The leader of that group, Ross, spent a lot of time helping me to understand that what happened wasn't right. Again, the heart battled with the head.

Ross was a wonderfully kind man who helped me begin the transition into the truth. He reminded me of Pa in a way – kind and gentle. He offered me a safe place to share what was deep inside. Sometimes that's all people need. He never professed to be able to 'fix' my issues. He never really gave me advice on how to work my life. He was just there.

A beacon. Another angel at the end of the phone line who cared enough to listen. At times, I would ask him why he bothered taking the time to help me. His explanations were simple but powerful. I thank God today that he took the time.

After several weeks of sessions with that group, I began to notice that people weren't turning up. Particularly the men. I noticed, but didn't care too much about it. Apparently, a couple of the men contacted Ross and explained why and I was asked to consider that these guys had dropped out of the group because I was so angry towards them.

This was very hard to swallow. I remember my head saying, *"What the hell do you mean? I don't even talk to them"*. (I probably even said that out loud as well – I'm not sure now). I wanted to deny this with everything I knew. *"How could they blame me? Isn't this their stuff?"*

The truth was, I didn't speak to them, but my *energy* was dismissing them in a very angry way. I could have justified all of this and kept up the fight, but I trusted Ross somehow, and I knew he was telling me the truth.

The guys came back and we talked about it, and I saw very clearly how I had made them feel extremely uncomfortable just with a look. Dismissing their existence, almost. This was a huge learning.

I am not alone in this behaviour; I'm just the one being honest about it. I see it happen constantly with clients, but often it's this underground energy that we deny. If we are not saying the *words*, we don't have to own anything.

I worked on my relationship with these guys and we got to know each other a little better. They were nice guys – this was definitely my stuff to work with.

That was the beginning of another big step for me. It wasn't necessarily about beating up my father. It was about me understanding my feelings. The feelings that had been shut down for years.

In my work today, I don't do 'parent bashing'. It's pointless, and only creates continued resentment. After all, we do create our own reality. If any resentment or anger exists, there is no clear place from which to understand Love.

It's my belief that we are here on this planet to understand unconditional Love. To find the strength to be who we are in any given moment. To find an unshakeable self-worth that brings about the contentment to love yourself and others from a real place.

What I see most in the world today is conditional Love. The layers of confusion and anger, plus every other emotion that is covered up in these situations, are a work in progress to remove. The day with my father allowed this process to begin for me.

Oh sure, I'd done lots of courses and read lots of books and listened to lots of speakers about how to deal with these shut-down feelings. I'd done university courses on how to help others. I was even in the business of helping others myself, working at a Boys' Home.

But I know today, very, very clearly, that there is no way through but through. The layers have to come off if you are going for reality and Love. It doesn't mean you need to revisit every past incident or be a victim to your circumstances. There is another way.

The way through this is by real connection. Real communication. There is nothing like connecting with another human being from an absolutely clear and true place. Nothing like it for allowing the process to unfold.

Most people want to help you to 'fix it' – to push you through it so they don't have to feel anything for themselves. Judge you for going through it. Have an opinion about how you should go through it. Become a martyr and 'do anything they can to get you to the other side'.

It's all poppy cock!

Most of that is about the person on the other end looking good. Feeling that they've done 'the right thing'. Point-scoring. Ego-based garbage, really.

I've experienced it many times. It doesn't help at all. In fact, if you're giving anything to anyone else and you have an attachment to the outcome, or if you have an agenda for any of the above things...then it is not giving at all – it is taking.

When you experience someone who is not in it for any reason other than to connect with you from their heart, then that one moment in time is worth a thousand 'do-gooders'.

8

Stories from the Grandfather

There is always a beacon of light.

My grandfather was the beacon of light in my life that proved to me, over and over again, that there was immense love to be felt, trust to be developed, and that we all had an innate connection with Nature that would sustain us in our times of need. That each one of us had a place inside ourselves that we could rely on to find peace.

It was the place I turned to when everything else failed. My backup. I don't remember a lot of talking going on between Pa and I during these times, just feelings – feelings that I could hold onto when the nights themselves were cold and unfeeling.

Pa was a simple man. He was also the man who taught me the greatest truth and the greatest humility I would ever learn.

Three steps down to Pa's place. Those three steps were often what I looked forward to the most. I clearly remember the feeling of taking those steps, quietly and quickly, while the rest of the house slept. Melbourne winters are notoriously grey, cold and drizzly. It was on those mornings that I loved this trek the most.

Down the steps, across the wet, cold concrete, heading for the doorway to the makeshift bungalow that was once our garage. Peeking through the door to make sure I wasn't disturbing Nanna and Pa. Always finding them up and waiting for me. This felt like the closest thing to heaven I knew.

Nanna would be busy stoking the fire – the smell of baking still to this day brings that memory clearly into focus. The warmth from the fire paled in significance to the warmth that radiated from my grandfather.

Pa knew what went on in our house. I know he knew, because sometimes on those mornings, he would take me outside into the elements and we would wander around the veggie garden. Or sit by one of the huge trees that surrounded our property. Or maybe go for a wander in the paddocks behind it. Nothing was really said on those mornings. There was just a look he would give me. A feeling I got from him that it was all going to be okay, just as long as I could find that place in me from where everything stems.

At other times, we would sit by the fire and he would talk to me about flowers and birds. The sky and the trees, and why these things were so important to us. Why, when we felt lonely or sad, we could find solace by being in Nature. He taught me that we would never be alone if we were surrounded by all that power and beauty.

He spoke of being true to yourself. Finding out what you believed in, and believing in that with all your heart. He had been a farmer in his younger years, and he had an immense passion for the land and gardens and putting back into the earth – the earth which is so generous with its gifts when properly taken care of.

He spoke of never taking anything for granted – of appreciating everyone and everything that crosses your path for whatever reason.

It was on those mornings spent with my grandfather that I gained an immense love for Nature and all its power and beauty, from the smallest of insects to the birds and trees, right through to the power of a storm and what it had to tell.

We watched families of birds and how they worked together to protect their young. Today, that is still a favourite pastime of mine. Now I teach my own grandchildren about the cycle of life. When they sleep over, I often sit on the verandah with them at dawn, wrapped up in blankets, listening to the world wake up. Listening to the chirp of the first bird, watching the night sky change slowly to light. Feeling the peaceful night energy change into the active energy of the day.

It's a very special time. I cherish those moments of allowing them to feel the wonder of Nature for themselves. No need for words – just letting them feel it for themselves. My daughters put up with it now. At first, they didn't want the sleeping patterns of the children interrupted, and I respected that. Now, as I creep out of bed before dawn to greet the day myself, there is often a patter of tiny feet following me to the door.

As a teenager, I was headstrong and wilful, and fought hard to get my point across. I felt a strong sense, deep down, that I was fighting for a lot more than that. I always knew there was *more*. I searched for things that would make me feel strong and passionate as my grandfather had shown me – the difference being that my grandfather was a gentle, passive man and for me, until now, that didn't seem to be enough.

I was in my thirteenth year when my mother announced that we would be going to hear somebody speak at the library of the local primary school at Kilsyth. I was less than impressed and fought pretty hard not to go. I had what I saw as good arguments not to go, and worked on those vehemently, my head justifying these arguments constantly. But somehow, something inside me knew that I actually needed to be there that night.

I found myself sitting in the midst of a packed house. As much as I grumbled and groaned, I felt a stirring inside that I would learn something very valuable to me. Onto the stage came what I considered to be an 'old' Aboriginal man. Well-dressed, a shock of grey-white hair and the kindest eyes I've ever seen.

I sat transfixed as this man, Pastor Doug Nicholls, spoke for two hours about the plight of the Aboriginal people in Australia. His voice was calm and yet passionate. His demeanour was compelling to me. I'm sure if the audience had been filmed, my mouth would have been visibly open in awe of this amazing man. I don't remember everything he said that night. For me, it wasn't about what he said. It was about how he felt. How I felt with him in the room.

The one thing I do remember was his speech

about his people not wanting a lot, but wanting to be able to walk beside us – to hold their heads high and be accepted for their differences. He asked the audience to hold aside their judgements of behaviour, and accept him and his people, without prejudice, for the Spirit that they were.

My heart burst forth with emotion I hadn't ever experienced. This tough little teenager sat and cried copious tears, listening and feeling the depth of this man's compassion for his people. His absolute commitment, in his life, to make a difference even to one other life. If only he touched one person, he said, "... I would die a happy man."

I walked from that room with tears streaming down my face. As I headed for the door, many, many people were milling around Doug Nicholls to ask questions. My feeling was they just wanted to feel this level of compassion up close.

I moved out into the corridor to go home and, as I did, this gentle man walked up beside me and put his hand on my shoulder. I turned around to look into those warm loving eyes and he spoke to me about the meeting of two souls. He told me that he had felt me in the audience and that we had connected at a warm safe level. He also said to me, "You will work with my people. It is in your heart that you will."

That night changed the direction of my life forever.

Oh sure, it got lost a bit over the years – I forgot about it from time to time. However, every time it came back to me, it was at one of those choice point moments in life, when I'd be standing at the crossroads wondering which path to take.

From both my grandfather and Sir Doug Nicholls, I learned the lessons of passion and truth. I learned to find what was true, and to fight for it. Not fight as in human terms. But fight from my Soul. The only true, strong place you can ever fight from. My grandfather had what he saw as little claim to fame. Doug Nicholls had moderate claim to fame. Both of them loved deeply, and embraced the simplicity and beauty of connecting with another human being at a deep Soul level.

Many years later, when I was travelling around the outback of the Northern Territory, I walked into a pub at Mataranka. This gorgeous little pub is actually a tin shed in the middle of nowhere. As I walked through the door with some colleagues from Katherine, I noticed an Aboriginal guy sitting in the corner on his own. I immediately felt the same connection as I had with Doug Nicholls – from that heart place.

We sat down on the other side of the bar and I didn't look back over, as I know that, in that part of

Australia, there is a lot of prejudice. In fact, one of my colleagues was openly racist. The altercations I had about this very subject during my time in the Territory and, also, in North Queensland when I lived there, could fill another book.

As we ordered our drinks, this man got up from his seat and walked over towards me. As he was approaching, I had many strong comments from the people around me, such as, "Don't speak to him, he's coming over to you ... you can't speak to him. It's not allowed here." Such comments only served to make me more determined to do what I felt. I watched him as he approached, and he was clearly very nervous about walking into the middle of all this hatred. I got up and met him in the middle of the bar.

He said, simply, "I felt your heart. You are connected to my people".

We sat together in the bar, to the outrage of many, and had a great talk about life and Spirit and connections – connections like that one, in which it would be so disrespectful not to speak, for whatever reason. He spoke about his fear of approaching me, but said his fear was not about me, because he had felt me. It was only about the others.

I left feeling a connection with another human being that was real and wonderful. That night, the people I was staying with in Katherine threw me out of the house in the middle of the night – literally got me out of bed and said they wouldn't have me there if I was going to speak to Aboriginals in pubs, or anywhere else for that matter. I left, and I had to respect their strong views on the subject.

As I watched this guy ranting and hurling abuse at me, I felt a real sadness that his journey had not thus far allowed him to connect with anyone from a real place. Especially himself. That his hatred and control – and mostly his fear, kept him locked in anger and resentment.

9

Real Connections

WE'VE LOST THE ART OF CONNECTION THROUGH all the learning we've done.

Does that sound tough? I hope so, because I believe it's the absolute truth.

It was not facts or information that I learned from any of those men. I don't remember most of the words that were spoken to me, really. All I remember is the feeling of connection, and the freedom to be exactly who I was in that moment without judgment. Without anyone trying to 'fix' me or tell me what to do, even energetically.

We had a funeral last week for 'Stripey', my four-year-old granddaughter Chelsea's goldfish. Chelsea had been away on holiday in Queensland with her family, and I had been fish-sitting. Unfortunately, Stripey had an attack of 'swim bladder'. I did my best, but he went to God overnight.

When Chelsea arrived the next day to spend a few hours with me, I told her about Stripey and she handled it very well. She said it was okay.

We set about making him a card and, as she wrote her message about being happy to have had him as her pet and how much she was going to miss him, she put her hand to her forehead and said, "Oh no, Nan! Oh no! I'm getting the crying feeling. I knew I'd do this!"

I tell this story because, at that moment, all Chelsea needed to do was *feel*. Nothing else. There was nothing I needed to say. Two of my team members, who had been assisting with card writing, were standing there, with tears in their eyes.

Chelsea had a moment of just feeling. She would miss Stripey. There was no need for any of us to 'fix' that – make her feel better – tell her a story about how we'd lost a pet – tell her a story about where Stripey was going or how he'd get there. We didn't need to do one single thing except support her moment.

I have been around death a lot, and not only goldfish. In my experience, it is something that people find very difficult – allowing another person a moment without trying to do anything but support. Support. Now there's a word. I'm talking about energetic support. Not the 'support' that I see in play in the world when people are in need.

Just to finish the Stripey saga – Chelsea had her moment of sobbing, and she and her sister Lucy picked flowers to put on Stripey's grave (which Chelsea had dug herself).

As we reverently stood around the grave, my two-year-old grandson, Heath, turned on a stereo at full volume, right behind us, and started dancing. It frightened the dickens out of us, of course, but it allowed Chelsea to move to another place. We all joined in the dancing and concluded Stripey's part of Chelsea's journey with a wonderful and very loud wake.

Supporting from a true place is something that I work with a lot in workshops, and I constantly see clear examples of people's muddled ideas of support.

I witnessed an elderly woman fall when leaving a shopping centre one day. She was walking along in the car park and didn't see the speed hump. I was driving towards her and watched, almost in slow motion, as she stumbled on the speed hump and literally flew forward, arms flailing. I got to her as she hit the ground, face down on the concrete. The poor darling was crying, and so shocked and afraid. Her first words were, "I'm so embarrassed!"

I sat down on the road beside her and asked her to just keep still for a moment, and I gently rubbed her back. There was a Doctor's surgery in the shopping centre, so I knew I could get her help straight away, but the main thing for me then was to settle her panic. As I rubbed her back, she started to settle down.

Suddenly, from out of nowhere, another woman who had witnessed the incident came barrelling over. She literally pushed me out of the way and started to lift the elderly woman up off the ground. She asked question after question: "Are you okay?" "Do you want me to get the doctor?" Then, without even leaving the poor dear space to reply, she launched into a story about her own mother having a fall and breaking her hip and ... blah blah blah. The whole thing became about her.

She dragged her off the ground, dusting her off while the poor lady just looked dumbfounded, saying, "...just get me to my car". This thoughtless woman just bundled her over to the car, popped her in the driver's seat and walked off, quite satisfied she had 'done the right thing'. I'm sure she'd be telling the story to her friends about how she had done such a good turn that day.

She was wrong. That woman did not *for one minute* think of the elderly woman. Her mind was running the show. Not her heart. I walked beside and watched as she shoved the elderly woman into her car, and I could see that the poor woman was still in a state of shock as she started to drive away. It was clear her shock had not been dealt with. What the interfering woman did, by her actions, was to pull the injured lady 'out of her moment'. Instead of supporting the moment and allowing her the space to feel what she needed for herself, the moment was completely railroaded by someone else's agenda.

One of my team members asked me why I didn't intervene. Believe me, it was very close to the surface. However, watching the bewildered look on this poor woman's face, I knew that my intervention would have caused another trauma that she clearly did not need. I could have gone into competition and told this woman how badly she'd handled it, but that would have made it about us and, again, not about the woman who'd had the fall.

 I believe that this is what is stopping people from reaching their own Knowing. Their own truth. It's that over-concern. The heads running the show with all their stored information, instead of allowing everyone to feel and know what is right for themselves.

I can hear some of my colleagues in the healing profession saying: "But people don't know what they need." The only reason they don't know is because 'others' keep telling them they don't. 'Others' keep having an opinion, and usually a strong one about that person's life.

10

Place in the Boat

"I was raised to sense what someone wanted me to be and to be that kind of person. It took me a long time not to judge myself through someone else's eyes". *Sally Field*

There was a place inside me that knew, instinctively, when my beautiful children were born that ... Yes, of course I needed to protect them. Yes, of course I needed to feed and clothe them. Yes, of course I needed to teach them what I knew to help them grow.

The other thing I knew, instinctively, was that I needed to teach them about their Place in the Boat.

As my two beautiful girls and my precious son were born, I brought each one of them from my womb, looked into their eyes and told them:

"I love you. You will never know the confusion I have known. I will tell you the truth to the best of my ability. I will walk beside you, not in front of you. Whether your memories are beautiful or painful, I will help you to find that place inside you that will grow from each experience. I will teach you that you have a place in this boat called Life. Do not let another person take the place that is yours. Once you understand that you need to hold for that Place in the Boat, you will never again question who you are and what you are here to do."

There is a connection made between parents and children from a place of truth that is unshakeable. Connected, yet not co-dependent. Caring for each other, yet living individual lives.

My kids went through all the normal childhood stuff. Yes, things happened that were not your normal, 'run-of-the-mill' family situations, but I believe that the learning for kids is always the same. To develop a sense of yourself in this day and age of competition is a challenge for any young person growing up. My kids were no exception.

I married young, without much thought about what I was really getting into. I didn't know how to be a wife – I barely knew how to be a teenager. I learned lots from the people I hung out with. Michael was a great guy and still is.

Rick and I married, and our beautiful children were a part of that relationship. Although we were like two bulldogs at each other's throats (not very sustainable), the one thing we shared was the love of our three kids. Even during the break-up of that relationship, there was a fierce need we shared, and completely agreed upon, to keep them safe. The trauma of marriage break-up is real, but we did our best to keep our fighting to ourselves.

When I see young couples now having difficulty sharing children in break-ups, it always brings to mind the feelings from my own experience, when Rick would bring the kids back from a weekend away and gleefully have them tell me, on the front step, that they'd "had McDonalds three times" and eaten steak for tea. The kids had been vegetarian for some years, under my strict regime of health and fitness.

Yes, of course I wanted to yell and scream and hit him very hard but I had promised to do this as nicely as possible for the kids. So I'd smile and say, "That's great guys" (with my heart pounding out of my chest and my anger rising). It didn't mean I wouldn't ring him when they were in bed and do a bit of yelling then, but I soon learned it wasn't worth the effort.

Eventually, Rick and I got through the worst of our resentment towards each other – resentment for who knows what, really? What it all boils down to is the fact that we just couldn't live together. At that time, I didn't have the skills I now have to assist couples to reach a truer connection. I don't have a clue whether that would have worked for us or not. It doesn't work for everyone. My only coping skill back then was to leave.

It didn't take us long to step aside from our own petty issues and do what we could, often together, to assist our children. Whenever there was a problem with the kids, he was the first one there to help. Our lives were completely separate as individuals then, but his love for his kids never wavered. I was, and still am, immensely grateful for that.

My son Tim said to me one day, some months after the separation, "It's so great that you and Dad have separated. Now I see Dad, and he's happy, and you're happy. It was horrible when you lived together – we could feel the tension." He was ten or eleven at the time.

As I said, we tried very hard not to fight in front of the kids, but they're not stupid. They feel everything that is going on. There were many nights that I looked at them while they slept and thought of staying – 'for their sakes'. It would have been an absolute illusion.

The agreement Rick and I had to keep them out of our conflict allowed them to stay solid within themselves, even if they felt upset or afraid. There was a place with each parent that they could come to and share their feelings, without being judged or told that the other parent was bad. It was a space for them to feel what they needed to, and to be able to make their own choices and have their own opinions without being ridiculed.

There were times I would have liked to have said, "Your father is behaving like an idiot", but I never did that. I never put Rick down to his children. They needed to find out what their own relationships were with him, without any interference from me. He allowed them the same space when it came to me.

We had some laughs at times, about what we wanted to say about each other, but it was never said to the children. Again, we were giving them the ability to make choices about how they felt without any influence from resentful parents.

From feeling their Place in the Boat from this early age, all of my children have developed a deep sense of themselves, and the Knowing they experience is profound.

In fact, these days, during workshops, I will bring both of my daughters in for a session or two, and learn enormous amounts about the people in the room from their intuition.

I made loads of mistakes that are clear to me now. I was fiercely protective, which I now believe didn't serve them all the time. I was fairly controlling – my need, I think, to keep them safe. It's been a big journey for me to understand that I was responsible for their safety as children, but once I overstepped that, it became control.

Both of my daughters, now mothers themselves, have pulled me up sharp when I've given little comments about their children in different situations. An example comes to mind from their first holidays, when both families, in turn, went to the beach. Before I knew what was coming out of my mouth, I had said to Niki and Damian, "Oh, watch out for Toby, don't leave him near the water alone". As soon as I'd finished the sentence, I heard the little voice that sometimes sits on your shoulder, saying, "Be quiet, this is none of your business". Too late – it was out. Niki, in her usual hilarious style, replied, "Mum, actually, we thought we'd tie a brick to his leg and throw him in." I was duly put in my place.

Imagine my surprise when, months later, Peta and Luke were taking their daughter Chelsea to the beach for the first time, and I said the same thing. I got exactly the same response from Peta. Thank God for my children's fearless responses to anything that steps over their boundaries.

With Tim, it's usually a look. I tried a few times to be overly motherly when he was going overseas by himself. Naturally, while he was away, every disaster that could happen occurred in the exact area he was travelling through. When I'd ring or email frantically to check on him, he would give me his own unique response:

"Keep it real, Helen".

Tim's grade four teacher came to see me one day, to relate a story about him that blew her away. One wet day, the kids were eating their lunch in the classroom, as was the policy on rainy days. There were lots of complaints from kids that the lunches their mothers provided didn't suit them. They wouldn't eat this or that, and weren't given what they really wanted.

Tim stood up in front of the class, and told them to stop moaning and start taking some responsibility for themselves. "If you don't like what you're given, then make it yourselves". Which is what he did. He also told them that, by making their own lunches, "It leaves you no one to blame but yourselves".

As they were going to the playground that day, Tim walked over to the teacher's desk and quietly asked her if she had PMT. He had noticed she was a little edgy, and said he recognised it because he lived with his Mum and two sisters, so understood the whole thing pretty well. He asked her if she knew that when women live together, their menstrual cycles often co-incide. "Imagine that?" he said. He suggested that she just take it easy over lunch, because that would help.

His teacher told me this story and conveyed that, really, she should have been shocked – or annoyed or something – that this nine-year-old had asked her about PMT, but he was so genuine that she simply said, "Thanks Tim".

I respect my kids immensely for their forthrightness, and their courage in doing the best they can in this life.

Obviously these kids have attracted strong independent partners as well – I'm as proud of Damian, Luke and Cassie as I am of my own three. They are friends I can count on. They give clear, direct and honest feedback if needed – or tell me they are not interested in being involved if it doesn't concern them.

There are so many stories that could fill this chapter, about the kind of adults my three children have become from the understanding they gained through being taught simple truth very early. Simple, yet, I believe, the most powerful understanding on the planet.

My intention for this chapter, in fact this entire book, is to reach people in the place that they can easily relate to. The place of real understanding, from which comes personal responsibility, personal growth and a life of fulfillment.

Cassie often gets frustrated with Tim, as he has never allowed people to say 'sorry' to him. His stand is that, if you do something, you've done it, and you meant it, and therefore don't bother apologising. When Tim went out on the town with the boys one night and had 'a few too many', he ended up in a bit of a scuffle with someone. A few weeks later, Cass was upset that people had been talking about him. Tim's attitude was the same, "I did it. I'm responsible for it. Let them talk".

My own Place in the Boat was often challenged as a child. My strong belief that people weren't always telling the truth got me into all sorts of hot water.

I had an aunt who constantly set me up to look like the bad child. It worked. I didn't like her and she didn't like me. They were the simple facts. However, she seemed to have the upper hand purely and simply because she was an adult.

One Christmas, she arrived with gifts for all four of us children. The other three were handed theirs one by one, with the ensuing build up to the unwrapping, where she held herself in high esteem for the thought she had put into the gifts for each individual. These were "Wow!" moments. My three siblings received the latest and greatest toys on the market at that time. The excitement built as she presented mine, but I knew from the beginning it would be something with far less value in a child's eyes.

I was correct. She handed me a small parcel which contained a book on something very boring. I told her I didn't like it, and spent the rest of that day in my room being told how bad and ungrateful I was. Maybe so, but I knew she was smugly satisfied with her efforts.

Nowadays, of course, I know that it's the thought that counts, etc. However, I still know in my heart that her motives were not pure or driven from the love she professed to feel for us that day. That there was a large element of manipulation in her actions, was as clear to me at ten as it is today.

11

The Need for Foundation

I'D LIKE A DOLLAR FOR EVERY TIME I'VE HEARD FROM A PARENT that they are simply controlling their children because they 'love them and want the best for them'.

Recently, I questioned one of my clients about why she continued to 'help' her child with her homework. There was one particular situation where this mother sat up until 3:00 am or some ridiculous time to complete the homework due in the next day.

Her response was that she was just trying to help. We explored that a little bit. I pushed under there just a tad and, of course, we ended up with the absolute conclusion that it had nothing to do with the child, but was all about the mother, and how she would 'look' to teachers or other parents if the child didn't hand the homework in on time or if it wasn't up to scratch. This example is just one of the many I've experienced about giving excuses for control.

We all want what's best for our children, but there are ways to give them the best you can without control and manipulation. The thing I recognize most in my adult children is that they don't have a need to 'people-please'. They have no fear of speaking up in any situation and they are spontaneous in their interactions. What they have to say is not always welcomed, but it is always honest.

During critical choice-point moments for the kids, it was important for me to know when to step in and support, and when to step out and leave them to it. Simple as that, really. Support from a place of allowing them to *feel* what's right for them, and giving them the space and back-up to feel strong about their decisions. Whether their decisions serve them or not, is their lesson entirely.

From my experience in working with many children and teenagers in the past few years, it's obvious we've come to a crossroads in how to bring them up.

From working in Social Services and hearing about the 'rights' of children, I feel we've missed the point somewhere.

We've given our children 'rights' without giving them the foundation from which to work – without teaching them about their Place in the Boat.

Which includes strong self-worth and an ability to read situations easily. It includes an acceptance that others are on a different journey, so that this Place in the Boat comes without judgement, and with the respect that others need to do whatever it is they need to do for their own learning.

Another one of Tim's classic remarks that fits well here is, "Whatever blows your hair back!" And the thing with Tim is he means that. He's not being flippant.

I see parents who are actually afraid to stand up to their teenagers for fear of upsetting them, which could have them 'out of control'. How do teenagers learn boundaries if they are given none? Trying to please them and keep them in control doesn't work and it never will.

I'm going to include a newsletter here which I wrote a couple of years ago. It's relevant.

What is it going to take, I wonder?

I have wondered many times this month what it's going to take ... to bring us closer as human beings doing this journey together on our planet for whatever space of time we are here ... and when we might look outside of ourselves and our little lives to extend something of ourselves to our neighbours, even to strangers.

I've had joyful moments this month spending time with my beautiful grandchildren. One of those moments was shared with a visit to an animal farm nearby. The joy of spending time with the children, watching them in awe of these precious little animals and showing them how to take care and be loving towards living creatures that are defenseless at such a tender young age.

Then to encounter others, there with their own children, pushing two- and three-year-olds out of the way ... literally... to gain front position for their own child to pat or hold these little animals.

If that didn't shock me enough, when the child/ children were FINISHED with the animal, I watched the week old bunnies and chickens being THROWN back into the pen ... so the child could move onto the next animal. It was much more than I expected to see or feel.

The question of course was why?

Why would people act this way? Why would people teach their children to use these living creatures for their own pleasure, and then discard them without a second thought? It was a huge effort for me not to be furious. I fought desperately against judgment.

After much thought and lots of discussion with the wonderful group of trainee facilitators that I work with, we decided there is so much to learn from this experience and it further reinforced our dedication to the job we are doing – assisting people to build real communities with real communication, to look truthfully at how we/they use their energy in any given moment of the day, to feel and be, rather than do and accumulate. Our job suddenly looked a whole lot bigger.

There were many ideas discussed and many logical and not so logical explanations. Mostly we came to the conclusion that people are so busy doing ...gathering possessions ...and just surviving, that we have forgotten how to live ... how to be.

Sounds simple doesn't it.

Question is how do we rectify this? How do we get people to feel again? It's obvious if we as human beings have forgotten how to feel then there would be no feeling for animals or any other living creature. It has to start with us. But so many of us are too busy to literally stop and smell the roses or watch a bird feed its' young or speak to someone just for the heck of it.

There are challenges to be faced.

It made sense then, in a way, that people pushing other children away to get their own child's needs met, must be feeling like the child is missing out somewhere. Perhaps it's the guilt of too many hours spent working and not enough "being" time with the kids that drives people to do such things. When they get to a place like an animal farm, it seems to be about getting as many touches of the animals and experiences for the child, as quickly as possible. And then, of course, there are the photos to prove that it was all accomplished, and to make us feel satisfied that the child had indeed had his or her cup filled in some way.

For me, that is a sad reflection of where we are heading. The 'what's in it for me?' syndrome. ' I'll get what I want at all costs'. Of course, this story is about an animal farm but if you think about it, it's what we are faced with right throughout our society.

It's time to change that.

If this seems like a hard line, it is. We have become complacent. Too many times we are faced with these things and feel it is not our place to stand up and speak. So I ask myself,' if not me, then who?'

I am blessed to be working with the Muragai trainee facilitators on these and many other issues and watching over the months as they grow and change and begin to feel who they are in such different ways. They also, at the beginning of their time with Muragai, said things like, "Don't expect me to garden or do any of that nature stuff, it's not my thing". Imagine the excitement I felt last weekend as these 10 gorgeous people turned up, some just after dawn, to work tirelessly in the gardens creating the most beautiful areas for us to work in and then thanked us for the privilege of doing that.

We all have a responsibility to help change things on this planet. Don't you agree?

The only way to do this is to take responsibility for ourselves by learning how we are using our energy in our everyday lives, and how to make changes if necessary. Let's go into Christmas and the New Year making one small change, and then go for the big ones in 2004.

What is it you would like to change now? ...

... to assist you to open up and expand into the new year with passion and joy, for yourself and for others? Not how much money you want to make *or how you can lose 5 kilos before New Year (those things are important as well) but how you can personally change something about yourself that no longer serves you, your family or the planet.*

That's the challenge we put out to you today.

Have a fabulous Christmas and start to the New Year.

Helen and the Team.

www.muragai.com
info@muragai.com

12

The Sewing Class

POWER AND MANIPULATION START VERY EARLY IN LIFE UNLESS you are onto it. Which most of us are not.

IT'S COMPETITION AND CONTROL. POWER AND ego run rampant in our society. I see it everywhere I look. It is my wish that anyone reading this book will get a glimpse of the subtleties of this energy that plays out in almost every interaction people have. Yes, I said it was subtle. Subtle, and yet so damaging that every day it destroys precious relationships that could otherwise flourish.

A wise mentor once told me, "There are only two energies on the planet. Love and control. While there is control running, there is no real Love."

The subtleties of control are something I truly want to bring to the surface amongst the pages of this book. It's one of the many things crippling the world.

We humans have really reached a point where we have to take a good hard look at what's going on around us before our societies get too far out of hand. Before truly loving each other for love's sake is lost to us, and control and competition become all that our children and their children will know.

What we need to build is strong healthy self-esteem. With children knowing what their own choices are. What I see most often now is control and competition, which build huge destructive egos.

Thirteen is a delicate time in any teenagers' life. Mine was no exception. I had some issues going on, that's fairly obvious from the pages of this book. My first year at high school was pretty much about finding my feet. Learning the new rules of being a junior in school rather than a grade sixer and the 'big kid'. All part and parcel of normal growing up.

Part of our curriculum was Needlework. I hadn't

done a lot of that kind of thing – horse riding, tadpoling and football were more up my alley. The teacher was a young woman, probably twenty-five or so I guess. Of course, in high school, you have a different teacher for every subject, so feeling my way with each different personality was a job in itself. Miss 'Smith' seemed to dislike me for some reason. I probably talked too much in class, but I could never be really sure why.

This made her a challenge for me. In the beginning, I was nothing if not enthusiastic. I did my best to understand what was being taught and get the job done. Our very first project was what Miss Smith called a 'sample piece'. It turned out to be a small square piece of material measuring about 4"x 4". Our job was to embroider a pattern onto this material. *'Okay then. Can't be that hard'.*

I undertook this project with much gusto. Actually, I took it home and worked like a beaver to make it as 'pretty' as I could. This was a slightly weird concept for me as I wasn't a real 'girly' girl. I was more of a tomboy really. So this was new, but I liked it. It was a good feeling to create something I could show to my family. An achievement, really.

The big day came for marking our 'sample pieces'. I was ready and willing. I remember the day as clearly as if it were yesterday. I headed off to class early and was so excited about the prospect of being admired for my work that I even sat at the front.

Miss Smith started with some of the boy's work first. She complimented them on "a job well done", and said "good efforts for first timers" etc. Then a few girls in the class, who had obviously done this sort of thing before, produced amazing pieces of work with patterns on them I could never have imagined creating.

Anyhow, so far so good. I was still feeling extremely positive about my own piece. The time came for my design to be shown. Miss Smith picked up my material, held it up to the class and started to belittle me. She laughed at the 'mess' I had made of the sample and criticized my design, telling the other children this was the worst example of any kind of sewing she had ever seen. She went on and on about it, but by now I was not hearing any of the words. I was watching her mouth move as she stood above me with a smirk on her face I won't forget. I fought back tears for a minute or two, and then I felt the anger rise.

I stood up from my chair and snatched the sample from her hand. This was all she needed. She grabbed me by the jumper and started pushing me towards the room at the back of the class which housed the sewing boxes. I fought as hard as I could, but she was determined. I was shoved in there and the door was locked.

From that back room I watched her. I yelled at her to let me out. She laughed. Eventually I piled the sewing boxes up in front of the glass door so she couldn't see me. I felt like a caged animal. Humiliated, but by now mostly furious.

I maneuvered my way up to the windows, high above the shelves. I climbed out through the slats, down into the corridor outside, then went around and knocked on the door. She opened the door, realised it was me, and began screaming hysterically. This, of course, sent the class into fits of laughter, which only served to fuel the fire underneath Miss Smith. She dragged me off to the principal's office.

This battle between us went on for a year. I spent lots of time locked in the back room. I found many ways to escape and then enter the classroom again through the door. It drove her insane. She drove me insane.

Of course, knowing what I know now, I could have done many things differently. But as a teenager that was how I survived.

The bottom line was that there was nowhere we could connect. Miss Smith tried control and manipulation and I bucked. Simple as that.

On the other hand we had a Maths Teacher, Mr Van Tat. He was the strictest teacher in the school. Nobody liked him. People left his class because he was too hard on them. I loved him because I knew where I stood. He told me what he expected and I heard him. I did what he asked to the best of my abilities and he acknowledged me for that. I was no Rhodes scholar when it came to Maths, but all of the effort I put in, he supported. I was able to connect with him from a clean place with no manipulation on either side. This was a man I respected.

13

Tough Love from the Most Gentle Place

MUM WAS TAKING MURRAY TO A SCOUT MEETING. THERE HAD been tension for an hour or so and a few hints from my father that Mum may fancy the scout leader or something. Again the green-eyed jealousy monster reared its ugly head. Mum didn't really have anywhere to go with the conversation, it was probably easier to ignore it and just go.

They left and a short while later Peter and I were arguing about something petty and Pete slammed his bedroom door. My father came through that door like a steam train and went straight for Peter. We were teenagers by this time and Peter stood up and faced him. My knees went weak.

I screamed at them both. I couldn't bear the thought of what might happen if he took to Peter now. He started to hit him and I got in the middle. I screamed to Peter to run. He said "No" but I screamed at him. I turned around and looked him in the eyes and my look must have portrayed that I was seriously worried about how this could end.

He ran.

I faced my father for whatever was going to come. I didn't care at that point. My only thought was to save my brother. I got one of the worst beatings of my life. The jug cord whipped into my legs until they bled. A pillow was stuffed down my throat to silence the abuse I was hurling at him. And I was hurling it, let me tell you. Every word I knew and more came out of my mouth that night.

This night changed many things in our household. Firstly, my mother came home from her meeting to find me in my bed covered in blood and bruises. She flipped out. It was the first time I had ever seen my mother stand up to my father. I couldn't get out of bed but I heard her screaming at him that this was not going to happen again. The doctor came and checked me out.

We weren't to tell anyone. I couldn't tell my Pa. I was told it would only hurt him. So I avoided my Pa for what seemed like a long time. That was a very difficult thing for me to do. He was the one I wanted to cuddle me. He was the one I wanted to cry on. It was a confusing time and I know Pa knew what had happened. He also knew he couldn't interfere. He still cleaned my shoes for school. He still walked round the veggie patch with me, but I felt like I couldn't reach out to him now. He just held for me. He watched me and rubbed my head when I passed him. He would put his arm around me now and then, and I'd feel that connection but then walk away once more.

I didn't speak to my father for a long time. A really long time. He bounced around and tried to be nice but I was over it. I decided I'd take any consequence that came but I was not going to speak to him.

One of the things he did after beating us up was buy new things. Mum would get new fridges or washing machines. We'd get new clothes or bikes. This must have been a big challenge for him because this time I got my horse, Nugget. My holding out on speaking to him got me a horse. There has to be something in that.

I accepted my horse but still didn't speak to my father. Mum and Pa had bought him for me so I guess that was my excuse for accepting him, but the fact was they had bought him with my father's money.

Today, in the same situation, I would say "No, thank you" to the horse. But throughout my life I had to learn that withholding your energy from someone could very well bring results. It wasn't clean but I did use it until it was pointed out to me. Now I do my best not to play that game of manipulation. I see it so often with kids growing up in ordinary circumstances. They learn to manipulate and be manipulated and don't even know its happening.

The greatest gift from all of this was that my Pa just stayed there with me. He didn't try and force me to talk to him. He didn't do anything. He just held for me to come through and understand that I could find that place in me he'd taught me so much about that was just me. I could go back into Nature and find the strength to get on with my life. He stayed beside me without a word but with his heart open so I could feel him every time he was near. This is Tough Love at its best. Eventually I understood.

I was a pretty tough teenager by this time in my life and my greatest thrill was spending each Friday night at Nanna and Pa's place. They had a new house now and I would go and have dinner with them and sleep next to my Pa. We'd read together. He'd still brush my hair. These were precious times in my life.

As we grew older it became more difficult for my father to hit us. The belting I described here was the last time he raised a hand to me, and I believe the last time he raised a hand to my brother or any of us. He still hurt Mum at times but I remember one day when they lived in Lilydale, Peter was visiting and Mum had been hurt again the night before.

We were out in the yard and I saw my brother pick up an axe and walk into the kitchen. He stood there with a look I'd never seen in his eyes before. Peter is a placid guy with a great sense of humour, but he had taken all he was going to take. He held up the axe and said to my father. "That's it. No more. It's over. No more."

We all cried that day including my father.

It was over. He could no longer stand over us. He had no leg to stand on now. We were too old to belt. We were going to stand up for Mum.

I think after that Peter and I were called once during the night to take Mum out of the house. After that final night my father changed. He really did try and redeem himself. I didn't buy it much, but I know he made connections with my brothers and their fam ilies that lasted until his death. He and Mum were able to be friends in the end and she looked after him for a few months before he died.

What if my father had been able to find that true place inside him that was full of love and hope? Love and hope for himself so there would be no need to control another?

We all come here to learn. Perhaps before my father died he saw a way that could be different and learned some things about power and control. I never asked him but the night he died I did feel a difference in the old man before me.

This again is my story, but in everyone's lives in many different ways this scenario plays out everyday in our world.

14

Don't Knock Yourself Out

'LIFE IN THE FAST LANE' IS PROBABLY THE ONLY WAY TO DESCRIBE this part of my life.

Studying, bringing up teenage kids on my own, managing a Unit in a welfare institution – I used my mind for everything. There were schedules to be kept. Tight ones at that. Programs to be written, and then of course the study. Managing staff and keeping a tight rein on the resident clients at the Unit. Life was busy. When I look back on this period of my life, it's no wonder I created something to knock myself out.

It was a busy night in full swing. Staff flat out with difficult clients. I don't actually remember too many details about this time in my life; it sort of floats in like a cloud, and then floats out again.

I left the Unit to get a breath of fresh air, so I'm told. There was a large dark staircase outside the door. An hour or so had passed before the staff realised I hadn't come back. I was found at the bottom of the staircase unconscious, and my next vague memory is of waking up in a CAT-scan machine.

I had been struck on the back of the skull with a billiard ball. My short-term memory was apparently shot to hell. Nobody really knows the details of what happened that night, but over the next two years or so, my life took a complete 360-degree turnaround.

I went from being a high-flying manager to not being trusted in the house alone in case I left the stove on. I could no longer work in the same capacity – or at all for that matter. I could no longer read a book. I had no memory of what I had said five minutes or even one minute previously. I couldn't drive the car too much because, for a start, I couldn't remember where I was going. Then there were the red lights. I couldn't remember what colour they'd been once I went through them. The consensus of opinion was that I had acquired some sort of brain injury.

It's all very much a haze now. The straw that broke the camel's back was a letter written by a doctor to my children, enquiring as to whether my family wanted to put me into respite care to give them a break.

I packed my bags and 'went bush'. A saying I had heard from an amazing woman came to me and it stayed with me for the next few months: "I don't know where I'm going but I know I'm not lost". I lived by this saying for a long time. In fact I still do to this day.

I found some of my Aboriginal friends in the Outback and spent time searching again for my Soul. The feeling of letting go of my thought processes was very frightening and I spent a lot of the time panicking, trying to grasp onto something that felt real. Now I know that what was real was the feeling in my gut. My head was just trying to get me to play the game.

It's not necessary to go through the whole story of what happened after the head injury. Suffice to say, I learned enormous amounts about how destructive the mind can be. Tough way to learn it, but that's me – I'm a Mack truck kind of girl.

 When the mind is the only thing we rely on, how on earth do we find the true place inside us that is real? How do we know when our intuition is trying to tell

us something? How do we know when Spirit is trying desperately to get through to us?

When I work, I always say what comes from my gut, from my energy. If someone asks me three minutes later what I said back then, I have absolutely no idea. It's gone and it doesn't come back. The mind creates perceptions of how things are when in fact when you take the mind out of the picture, the truth is usually the opposite of what the mind is telling you.

Recently, in a group I was running, I asked the participants to refrain from reading any new books or literature for the upcoming four weeks. Four weeks is not a long time but the reaction from some members of the group was amazing. It bordered on panic.

There were comments like, "We learn a lot from reading". "We love reading. It helps us gain more knowledge" and "Do you want us to stop reading other people's work and just listen to you?" That was the key for me. I replied that I didn't want that, I just wanted them to listen to themselves.

We've lost the art of tracking down inside ourselves to find contentment and clarity.

 Think of all the people you know. Do any of those people who have decisions to make, particularly tough ones, just

make them from their own gut? Never asking an opinion from another? Never being indecisive? Never second-guessing themselves? Do you know any people who make choices and decisions with ease and grace and never have regrets? I don't know many people like that.

All the mind does is control. It's addictive. I knew that while I was spending time in the Outback, trying to work without constantly going to my mind for the answers.

The writing of this book is easy — since I pushed through my initial resistance to telling my story. The energy flows and I write or it doesn't and I don't. I can't force words onto a page. I don't really have them to force. It makes life very easy. I've found that the times when the energy shuts down and I can't write at all is when my mind is playing the old games, trying to get in and tell me things that aren't accurate. My mind tells me my story is boring and not worth writing or reading. The truth of what I *feel* is that if my story can assist one person to go to their Knowing with the courage to grab the brass ring, then the book has been worth writing.

So much of what I see in the world involves people holding themselves to a position or having a perception of themselves based on a lie that their mind is telling them. My guidance and intuition tell me on a daily basis that ninety-five per cent of the world's confidence is built on a lie.

I'll use an example I've worked with recently. Picture 'The Healer'. She runs her healing practice taking care of others and gathering people around her who adore her and see her as a higher being or something very special. This is all fine if this image of herself is built from the sustainable place inside her that is unshakeable. That means if she were challenged about what she was doing, there would be no rocking of her world.

Fact is, I did challenge her perception and she threw a tantrum for weeks. It may not have looked like a tantrum to the world, but it was a full-blown energetic tantrum. Her mind could not come to grips with the fact that she was using people to make herself feel above them or more 'whole'.

This gorgeous girl is committed to working on getting underneath her stories and getting to the truth of who she is. Then she knows she will be an awesome healer with so much to give. At the moment it's all about the taking. It's all about her and has nothing to do with her clients. This scenario is much more common than people would like to admit.

In another instance, I worked with a very high-profile corporate person who started the session by questioning me for almost an hour about my credentials, my experience and basically my life history.

I told him I'd completed many university studies, but that I'd thrown the qualifications in the bin, as I didn't agree with the philosophy. I said I worked with energy, getting underneath people's stories and that if he wanted to work with me we could work, otherwise I wasn't going to waste my time.

He agreed to go ahead. I asked him how he felt when he opened his eyes at 3:00 am. He went straight to his head about how many houses he owned, how much money he had and how successful his kids were. I held my energy. I didn't answer him, I just stayed silent.

When he finished raving on, I asked him the question again. He cried for a long time in that session. Cried for lost moments. Cried about the loneliness he felt as he drove up the driveway of his multimillion-dollar home, where the connection between him and his family had been replaced by status and money. This, also, is so much more common than people like to admit.

The dichotomies that run in the world alongside the confidence built on a lie theme are extraordinary.

15

The Aboriginal Connection

I HAVE A LONG HISTORY WITH THE ABORIGINAL COMMUNI-
TIES IN Victoria and Queensland. As a young woman
of nineteen, I met up with a family in Doveton, Melbourne, who had six children under six. I spent a lot
of time with them and over the years I had some of
the kids to stay with me for the holidays to help the
family out. As they got older, they lived with me for
some of the time.

Today, Cheryl, who was one of those kids, has a
son who lives with me full-time. Daniel is seventeen

and is training with a high-level football team. His dream is to play Australian Rules football professionally and I'm doing my bit to give him a shot. My dream is that during his intense training they also teach him how to clean his room.

My connection with these people has taught me many things. One very important lesson I've learned is that when Daniel's mood changes dramatically, then it's time for him to go to his people. In the beginning this was a bit tricky. Your average primary school doesn't really understand 'walkabout'. And the local football team found it difficult to understand why Daniel would disappear for a month in the middle of the season. For me they were times of finding a place to 'let go and let God'.

At times the home situation at his mum's was not ideal and she was battling to make ends meet. The prejudice that exists in his hometown of Bairnsdale is horrifying and I have experienced situations that make my blood boil.

For example, one day Cheryl was trying to buy medicine for one of her children who had just been released from hospital. The chemist was looking through her and around her before finally telling her he would not serve her because she was Aboriginal.

She came out in tears. I dragged her gently back

into the shop, pushed her up to the counter and asked her to order the medicine in a loud clear voice. The same thing happened. He looked through her and around her until I stepped out from behind her and glared at him. I looked him straight in the eye, willing him to take me on. He served her, but let me tell you, he was not a happy little bunny.

There are hundreds of stories like this, and many much worse with which I could fill a whole book. Maybe the next one.

The point is, as a mother myself, I did not want Daniel to go home to anything that was dangerous or out of control. I had no choice. I needed to feel what this boy needed and follow that. If I had tried to control him or make choices for him he would not be where he is today. He would have gone home for good and not had the opportunities he now has to further his career in football.

For Daniel, being supported by his family and mine to do what he needed to do, has made him aware of that very thing. His needs. When they are not blocked he is free to feel when he needs to be with his family. Then free to know when it's time to come back. He says for him he needs to feel a connection to his family to sustain him while he's here.

They live different lives to me. Their values are

completely different to mine. In the beginning I didn't understand why Daniel would go home with all his new belongings and come back with nothing. In fact, I'd be furious at his lack of responsibility. I learned quickly, with the help of his mother, that you just don't send the good things. Daniel would see a cousin or a friend without shoes or jeans or whatever else and give his clothes away without a thought.

Many people challenged me about just not buying him anything on his return to teach him a lesson. The thing is, Daniel couldn't care less about that. If he had one outfit to wear, he was happy.

The only way to deal with these things is for me to feel what is happening in each situation. Deal with it as it comes up. Hold strong boundaries and at the same time allow the flow between us and our differences to create a harmonious relationship.

The only way to deal with these things is for me to feel what is happening in each situation. Deal with it as it comes up. Hold strong boundaries and at the same time allow the flow between us and our differences to create a harmonious relationship.

I have been blessed over the last thirty-five years to be connected to, and spend much time with, many Aboriginal people all around Australia. Daniel's large extended family is no exception. In fact when I go to Bairnsdale these days with Dan there are sixty or more beautiful children who call me "Nan", which in itself is an honour.

Through these connections I have spent time in the bush with groups of Aboriginals who have taught me so much about the land that is our home.

During one of these times I started to get an insight into one of the things that I work with lots today. This particular group of people I spent time with worked in silence for most of the time. I'm talking here about a couple of weeks without using words.

A fair shock to the system for me. For them, it was all about knowing and understanding Nature and working within that without the interference of words.

It was also about them communicating with each other without the encumbrance of words. Communicating through their energy.

What an incredible gift that time turned out to be. At first I was frustrated that I couldn't speak and share my 'words of wisdom'!! What a joke. I soon learned I knew very little about anything much at all.

I watched and learned as these people went about their day without the mind chatter and all that entails. Astounding really – and fabulous training for me.

 I settled into this routine and began to 'feel'. A whole new world opened up. The world of energy. The world of silent communication.

Communication which was so much more effective than anything I'd ever experienced before....

16

Hayesy

I TALKED ABOUT DANIEL IN THE PREVIOUS CHAPTER, BUT IN hindsight the Daniel Hayes story is truly worth a chapter of its own.

He came to me as a scrawny little two-year-old with the biggest, darkest eyes I'd ever seen. Cheryl was struggling to make ends meet, Daniel had been sick for a while and a decision was made that he would stay with me and get medical attention until he recovered. That was the beginning of fifteen years of learning.

Learning for all of us I guess. Daniel's family. My own family. There were times over the next couple of years where he would go home for a few months, then come back to us and not speak a word for a week or so. It was usually his choice to come back, but the transition away from his own people and back to us was huge for him.

I had this idea that if we kept him connected to his family as much as possible via phone calls and visits (even though it was hours away), then we could somehow manage to keep him grounded.

I was completely wrong. Daniel dealt with it in his own way. We just had to observe and listen to him. My kids were great at picking this up. The three of them have amazing intuition and felt things in him I was missing through my concern to keep him safe.

It became very clear that the way he worked was that when he was with his family, he was with his family. No matter what went on there, it was just dealt with. He made no contact with me unless he was desperate to come back. Then, when he came back, he kept his family at arms length. There seemed to be no need for him to contact them at all while he was with us.

Obviously, this was his way of keeping the two worlds separate so he could cope.

When both families were together, Daniel found coping hard, as if his loyalties were being challenged or something. For me that was never an issue. His mum is his mum. He loves her, and I love that he does. He and I have a completely different relationship. I am his carer, and when things aren't safe and he feels it, he comes back to me. That's how it's always been. It works.

There have been times when Dan's gone home to Bairnsdale and simply because it's a town full of prejudice, I've received a phone call to say he's in hospital or he's been bashed up because of his skin colour.

These times are not easy. In fact they're tough. I have to pull in everything I know to just let it be. Not to go up there and chase whoever has hurt him. Or to yell at the people who didn't take care of him. I don't do any of that. It's his journey and he conveys that very strongly when he comes back. "This is my stuff, Nan. You have to let me do what I need to do."

In a way, Tim prepared me for this. Although the circumstances were different, he was so strongly self-sufficient he often said similar things, "Just let me do what I do, Mum."

It worked for him too. Tim – and Niki and Peta – know exactly who they are and what they need to do for their own lives. There isn't a lot of fuss. They just set about doing what they need to do.

With kids like Daniel, you definitely need to set strong boundaries when they are with you. What I provide for Daniel is a safe place to fall when he needs support, without the judgement.

When Dan was five, we enrolled him at Billanook Primary School in Montrose, Melbourne and he wrote a note in class that said "I will play AFL football for Collingwood". Funny really, because he doesn't like Collingwood as a team, his team is Essendon, but that's what he wrote. I know lots of young boys have that dream, but there was something in Daniel that just created circumstances to enable him to follow it.

He had a safe place to live with me. He was always well-liked by his teachers at school right through to his time at Lilydale High School. There, teachers supported him to stay on at school for as long as possible so that he could be with his mates. Despite the fact that the only real work he did there was to socialise. Dan has an incredibly strong bond with the mates he was with in primary school who accompanied him right through his high school years. He played with all of them for the Montrose Football Club from Under 10's days.

People love Dan and he gets looked after. Families in the area looked out for him and helped out with lifts to basketball and football while I was working. One of

Hayesy's best mates is a kid named Shane Hudson. The two of them have hung out together from a very early age, and Shane and his family were there during those times when Dan came back from Bairnsdale, confused and upset. Bev and Jeff helped a lot with Dan in those early years, and Shane was someone Dan could rely on. The boys have one of those close relationships that hangs in there no matter what – even though one or the other might throw the occasional tantrum, they will always find each other again.

Only the other night, the two of them were here, hair all slicked back, their aftershave smelling out the house, getting fires lit out on the back deck, putting drinks on ice and lining up just the right DVD's while they waited for the two pretty young girls who turned up to spend the evening with them. They've come a long way from the two scruffy seven-year-olds I took photos of, waiting for Santa outside our Montrose home ten years ago!

Last year Dan started playing football with the Eastern Ranges TAC Cup Squad and was very successful. He is now working for the AFL 'Sports Ready' program and works with the Ranges, assisting at kid's football clinics and lots of other fantastic things.

John Lamont, the Ranges coach, has been one of those angels that come along in life. John, together with Mark Heaney, the other angel down at the Ranges, support Daniel towards his dream. This is not always easy with Hayesy. He's gorgeous….luckily. He can also challenge the boundaries quite a bit. He has quite a simplistic way of thinking that if you see something you want to do, you just do it and everything will fall into place. Somehow for him that works and everyone supports him. But it's not always easy.

Not too long ago, in fact right before the season finals, Daniel decided he needed to go home for the weekend to Bairnsdale. My reaction was uneasiness, but knew I had to support him. John Lamont, I believe, held his breath waiting for him to come back. Here was a coach going into high-level finals (in fact Under-18 AFL finals) and one of his key players goes walkabout.

I think I mentioned John was an angel. As it happened, Daniel met with an unfortunate incident while away and his stay was extended a few more days. More breath-holding. Mine as well now. The phone call that came to tell me Dan had been beaten very badly by three thirty-year-old men had me crashing a little. I made a tearful phone call to John that evening, and felt one hundred per cent supported, by him and also by Harry, Lyn and Terry, some of the other parents who've been so wonderful with Daniel.

Lyn and Terry's son Scott, another of Dan's close friends, and a Ranges team-mate, wanted me to drive up there with him and get Daniel. I knew his fear but I also know there is no point to any of that until Dan rings to say it's time to come home.

A couple of days later he arrived home bruised and a little shut down. I let John know he was coming and within a couple of hours he had organised a barbeque at Mark Heaney's place to welcome Daniel back. To support him and let him know the Ranges staff and fellow players were concerned about his well-being.

It was an incredible thing for them to do and it assisted Dan to re-integrate quickly. The first final at Optus Oval in Melbourne took place the following Saturday. With a fairly bruised body Dan ran out on the ground with his mates and they won the game. Unfortunately for the other team, about half-way through the game one of the opposition players knocked Dan to the ground. I sat and cried as his mate Scott and many other members of the team ran across the ground to his aid. I don't condone violence, and it didn't go too far, but it did my heart good to see these boys saying energetically and with their strong bodies: "You are not going to do this to Hayesy". They took those kids on physically while Dan was picked up, given the ball, ran down the ground and kicked a goal.

I also cried when I read the match report from John later that week. He was warning the boys to be careful when stepping into a scuffle at this level of football, that it didn't end up turning the game around... he also mentioned that he was glad they "flew the flag for Hayesy".

Today, as I'm typing, Dan has hit a critical wall. His mum has gone walkabout for a while and he doesn't know where or how to contact her. His mind is locked into "Mum is coming to Melbourne to take care of me next year for the first time in a very long time", and for the moment, that plan has gone astray.

He was clearly upset this morning and didn't want to go to work. I didn't know about his mum at this stage, as I hadn't spoken to him about that. All I knew was that he wouldn't go to work and he wanted to go home to Bairnsdale. I was fully immersed in writing this book so I called Mark and told him what was going on.

Mark said they would come round and speak with him. Both John and Mark arrived at our home, went straight to Daniel's room and talked to him about what mattered and how much he needed to commit to his career etc. When they came out and asked me to make them a cuppa I told them about Daniel's mum. He had 'forgotten' to mention it (actually, it's not that he forgot to mention it, but in Daniel's mind he didn't want to be shamed).

When Dan came to sit with us, John mentioned his mum and what was happening. Dan was clearly mad at me for mentioning it, but they worked with him around him being able to open up and tell them these things, so they could help when he needed to go home to see his family.

We talked about needing to see family and about how we all knew when we would next see our own, even if it was a long time between visits. Dan didn't ever really know when he would next see his family, so when things went wrong he needed to go home and be with them. These guys understood and allowed Daniel the space to spend a few days with his family with a commitment that he would return for the start of the season on Sunday. The kind of support afforded Daniel in this Club is extraordinary. They go the extra mile.

Daniel's unending determination to play high-level football will most likely get him over the line, but I have to say he creates a path for himself with incredible support. I, for one, am very grateful to the people in Daniel's life who have not only supported him, but in doing that have supported me as well.

Once, I was in the middle of running an intensive

workshop at home. It was a seven-day intensive where people look at their 'stories' and work to get under them. There's often a lot of tension. Daniel is used to these situations. He lives with me, and the intensives often take place at our home.

This one morning, I walked out to the kitchen/dining area where a group of people were working on some very deep issues. Two of them were sobbing almost uncontrollably, sharing big stories about their lives and their grief. Others were intently supporting and 'being there' for these guys. I looked over at the kitchen bench where Daniel stood in his boxer shorts eating coco pops. His expression was one of bored indifference. It told me he'd experienced this kind of realness so many times before it really didn't mean an awful lot.

The other side of the coin is that during another one of these intensives, Dan decided to come home late with a couple of mates after a few beers. We had just purchased a small motorbike, which was all the rage at the time. He was very excited about his new bike and at sixteen, of course he wanted to show it off to his mates. From memory it was around 1:00 am. I and the entire team of people staying at the house get out of bed at dawn so there were only a few hours of sleep left for these already exhausted people.

I heard the boys come in and dozed back to sleep. The next sound I heard was the beeping of the motorbike horn. I rushed out, stepping over bodies as I went and found Daniel and one of the boys mucking around with the bike on the back deck.

I have an incredibly strong belief that God is watching over us, but that night I knew it more than ever.

I went back to bed and five minutes later the beep started again. I went outside, and both the bike and Daniel's mate were gone, and the beep was fading into the distance. Daniel was in his room with the other boy.

The next hour or so was chaotic and I have to tell you my neighbours must have had some fun listening to the ensuing games. Daniel told me the boy had taken the motorbike and ridden home. Home was many kilometres away and this boy had clearly been drinking. I was panic-stricken and went about trying to find his mother's phone number to call and let her know what had happened.

However, the workshop participants (who were all up by now), remarked that they could still hear the beep of the horn. It was 1:30 am. We all sat on the front deck listening. It turned out that the young fellow had taken the bike into the bushes next door to wait for Daniel, who was going to climb out of the window to meet him and take the motor bike for a spin. For the first and only time ever, the motorbike started to beep its horn each time the boy turned the handlebars.

All the while Daniel was telling me to calm down and not to worry. I *was* worried and let him know in no uncertain terms. In fact we came face to face in the kitchen. Now Dan's 6'1" and I'm not, but he was not about to challenge me any further that night. It reminded me of the many times when my own kids would say to me after a challenge, "There's a certain look you get in your eyes, Mum. Then we know the party's over, there's no more pushing the boundaries." Daniel must have seen that look, as he climbed into bed very sheepishly while we waited for the other boy to show up.

I can't imagine how frightened Pete was that night. There he was, stuck in the bushes, holding this motor-bike that kept beeping every time he tried to bring it back. Finally I heard the beeps coming closer to the house (he must have got tired of waiting) and I confronted him.

Pete has very white hair and that night his face matched his hair. He babbled about how he had been there all the time waiting, and he was visibly upset. I went a bit easy on him knowing how tough it must have been to have been hiding in the bush directly under the verandah where my entire team were sitting having cups of tea at 2:00 am. With a motorbike that just wouldn't shut up!

Although we've laughed about that night many times – and Dan's mates now laugh about it too – that night none of us saw the funny side. And who knows what might have happened if the motorbike had kept quiet?

A FOOTNOTE TO THIS CHAPTER:

As I mentioned earlier, Daniel had gone home for a few days to see his family. Whilst there he learned that his Nan, Violet, an Aboriginal elder and a very special lady not only to Daniel but to everyone, has just been diagnosed with tuberculosis. Violet has stood beside Daniel many times in his journey to AFL football. She is a keen Collingwood supporter, so she teases Dan a lot about his team, Essendon. She also spends her last dollar every Monday in the football season to see if her grandson's name is in the Herald Sun newspaper. I have spoken with her many times about her pride in what Daniel is achieving and I know she would be telling him to come back to Melbourne and follow his career.

This news is going to throw up a big choice-point for Hayesy. Family is all-important to him – particularly Violet. I'm praying now that he holds his dream tight and keeps walking forward.

I guess one more example of having to choose between the head and the heart.

A tough choice for Daniel.

17

Patience

Where do I begin to explain the lessons I have learned from having Hayesy in my life?

One of the biggest learnings for me was the fact that no matter what, you cannot control him. You can work with him – and he'll work with you to a certain level – and then that blank look comes across his face and you know that's it. No matter how much fear may arise in you at what he's proposing to undertake. *"That's it. Give it up now, the rest is a waste of energy"*. That learning has been invaluable and has saved me a lot of stress.

Bringing up my own three kids I could enforce different rules that helped us to get through the teenage years. For example: "If you want to stay out or go somewhere other than where you are supposed to be, just ring me and tell me. It doesn't matter what time it is, just ring". I think that's pretty standard in a lot of households. It worked well.

Given Daniel's background, when he's at home in Bairnsdale nobody asks where he's going or how long he'll be. In fact, when he was away last time, his mum called and when I asked how he was she replied, "Not sure, I haven't seen him for a few days."

We had to learn to juggle, Dan and I. " You bend a little my way Dan and I'll bend a little your way." It works pretty well (although I have to say I'm doing a bit more of the bending at the moment...). He still gets 'the wanders' now and again but most of the time he'll call and tell me. Not always. But most of the time. His friend's parents also call me to let me know when he's with them, even if he doesn't do it himself.

Communication was a big thing in our household. After Jo died there were lots of times I had to open up a forum for discussion with my kids, Jo's kids and any other kids who were around to make sure we all kept dealing with our grief.

As for Dan, he speaks a lot when he wants to.

When he doesn't want to he simply doesn't. He has everything running around his own head and lets you know when and if he feels the need to talk. It makes it a little tricky with pick-up and drop-off times given that I work full-time. Luckily, I work from home for the majority of the time which helps when he decides two minutes beforehand that he needs to be driven to work or home from work or to football training etc. Responsibility is one of the things we are all working on with Dan. It's a big mountain to climb.

Some months ago Daniel was asked to play an 'extra' in a movie. The casting agent also wanted a few other Aboriginal people so I organized for Cheryl, her twin sister Chris and some of the kids to come down and be in the movie as well. This was great; they all had a fantastic time and received a cheque for doing it. Fun all round.

After signing up all the kids, we sat on a beach near town somewhere, ate our lunch and shared some time together. Half-way through lunch I felt Daniel change and I knew something was coming. He knew Tim and Cassie were arriving that evening for their first visit from Queensland since moving up there some months earlier. They were planning to base themselves at my place and do their visiting from there. I was looking forward to this immensely.

As we all started saying goodbye before our respective trips home, Cheryl, Daniel's brother Wayne and his cousin Alex all started getting their things together and moving across to my car. I asked what was happening and was told that Daniel had asked them to come and spend time with him at my place. My first reaction was anger. I was furious with him for not telling me anything about any of this and I believe I was justified in feeling that way. I'd spent days doing the 'white tornado', getting the house spotless for Tim and Cassie.

I said this couldn't happen and was determined to stand firm on it. I looked across at Daniel and his face displayed absolute devastation. He was pale underneath his dark skin and had tears in his eyes. I took a breath and walked out to the water. I was still furious. But I also felt something else. This get-together we'd had with Daniel's mum that morning was probably the first time in a very long time the two of them had connected like they did. I'd watched as he lay on the lawn while his mum rubbed his back and I'd seen the look on his precious face.

Most of Daniel's trips to Bairnsdale were spent with his Aunty Chris, as Cheryl had been struggling a lot in the last few years. They hadn't communicated a great deal and this new feeling for him was something he was trying to hold onto a little longer. I sat looking at the water trying to feel what was right. My own son would be arriving soon expecting to stay and they couldn't all stay.

From somewhere I knew I had to let them come. I put a little clause in that I would allow Cheryl and Wayne to come but not his cousin. It just felt like making a stand, I guess, but it turns out that it worked well. Cheryl and I spent time sitting at my place looking at the native bush. They stayed for a week and Cheryl looked at her life from a different perspective – from the love Daniel was so warmly offering her.

How did Tim handle it? As Tim does. I could have fought from my head with the thoughts (probably justified) that Tim and Cassie had planned to stay with us, had organised everything around that plan and that you can't just change those things, especially not without telling me.

It was deeper than that. Tim and I have experienced millions of those connected moments and always will. No matter where Tim has been in the world I feel connected to him as he does to me. I called my daughters to ask whether Tim and Cass could stay with them, and they both said "Of course". I rang Tim as he got off the plane to tell him what had happened and his response was, "Whatever blows your hair back Helen. It's just a bed; we'll see you tomorrow."

For Daniel and Cheryl it was a connection that's taken them much further in their relationship.

So, did I give something up? No, not at all. We all gained.

18

The Deeper Truth

SOMEWHERE AMIDST ALL THE 'STORIES' OF MY LIFE, THE ONE
thing that became glaringly obvious was my fear of
stepping into being a woman in my own right. Especially if I look at it from the 'mans world' take on
relationships.

Sure I'm a good mum, good nan, good foster nan
to Daniel and to some of the others that have needed
help over the years. I believe I'm reasonably good at
being a daughter to my gorgeous mum. She and I are
friends and that's a great achievement. We spend time

together and we find time to take holidays together when we can.

I've done my very best with Jo's two kids. I've had a lot to do with them over the years and they are a very special part of my life. I don't see Matt much these days, but when I do it's gorgeous and our connection is still strong.

I'm an average sister to my brothers, Peter and Murray. We have our own brand of unique relationship. I'm maybe a less-than-average sister-in-law to Georgina and Kerrie and a less-than-average aunty to Nick, Lee, Ami and Scott. Then there's Peter and Connie. Peter is Matt and Kate's father and Connie is his wife. After Jo's death we all had to work together pretty closely to help Matt and Kate out the best we could. Peter and Connie have their own daughter, beautiful Bonnie who is now ten, a very special sister to Matt and Kate and a very special part of our family as well.

I love them all dearly and we are all very different people. I respect their differences and when we catch up it's always the same – easy. We don't see each other often – there's no pressure between any of us to 'keep up appearances'. Occasionally we feel the need to connect around Christmas and that's great. But it's not a 'given'. However, if any of my family needed me for anything I would be there in a second.

I've developed the skill of being a good and compassionate boss to my staff. That happened after I got over trying to take care of them and be responsible for them, and let them take care of themselves in the work situation.

I'm a great teacher and counsellor. I can help anyone get under their stories if they are game to sit in front of me and be exposed.

I have been a so-so partner to Michael, Rick, Doug and Arch, the significant relationships of my life. 'So-so' meaning that I did the best that I knew at the time of each relationship with the skills I had.

On reflection there was lots I didn't know. It's been an amazing unfolding since being single again this time to feel some deeper truth about why I have chosen at particular times to go into relationships. How they pan out, what I've learned from each one and whether or not I carried the same baggage into the next one.

At the end of our relationship, Arch and I knew it was simply over. We dragged it out for a year or so doing the co-dependent shuffle – you know the one…."*How will I get Daniel to football three nights a week as well as working full-time if Arch moves back to Queensland? Who will mind the dog when I have to go away to work? Who will cook dinner when I've worked for eighteen hours straight?*

What about the lawns, and the gardens, and the fish that need feeding?"

Of course that was all about me and a convenient lifestyle. For each of us, it was about using the other to stay where it was comfortable, despite the fact that I knew my life had never really been about 'comfortable'. Arch also hung on as long as he could, but we both knew it was time to move on from each other. We'd learned a lot and shared a lot and we are still great friends but our time in relationship was done.

Sitting here today, I believe a lot of what has taken place throughout my life has led me to shut down that vital part of being a woman. That part which is so important and which is often lost in our struggle to survive intact.

The struggle is not just about surviving all the roles we decide to play. It's then also dealing with whatever particular issue we decided to take on as kids or teenagers, dealing with the environment we were brought up in, dealing with the media and their 'take' on what men or women should be.

 There is so much that challenges us not to be whatever it is we feel is right for us.

I am great at standing up and fighting for so many things in my life, as you have probably already guessed from reading the pages in this book. I am only just beginning to learn how to fight for me, just *me*, as a woman in this world.

I see hundreds of women with the 'empty nest' syndrome. Once the kids leave home they are lost, as they don't have a role. There are books being written on the topic all the time. I also see lots of men who hit forty and the 'Where's my life gone?' feeling hits home. The roles we play often cover up the truth of those essential parts of us that remain dormant unless we're game enough to pull off the blanket and have a look.

We live in relationships and we survive. Lots of us survive well. It all looks great, but I'm guessing we compromise that deep intimate connection for the roles we play. For looking good, being right, being in control of another, being controlled by another or any other number of things that come under the category of survival. For some reason, all of these things make us feel safe, but it's not true safety. It's co-dependent safety.

I had an experience this year mixing with some of Melbourne's elite. Great people. No real connection with each other. I watched couples who held hands and smiled at each other a lot. They shared a pride in their children, they had status, money and everything that the world envies but they had no real connection from that deep place of sharing. None.

Peta and I were flying to Canberra with our neighbours, Cass, Mick and their kids for a few days holiday. I had been flat-out at work and I was looking forward to the rest. Men were definitely not a part of my life during that time. I'd been separated from Rick for years and life was all about work and kids. Just for the record, I was very happy about that.

The trip had a very weird beginning. I was in a state of panic before we even got on the plane. It was something I couldn't really explain. I fly often, but the sight of the small aircraft on the tarmac threw me into complete chaos. I had fear running rampant inside me and I couldn't understand it at all. Peta was looking at me with a strange expression on her face, wondering what on earth I was up to. I couldn't tell her, I didn't know. I even insisted on seeing the pilot to make sure it was okay to fly on that small plane in rough weather. What a joke! His reply was, "If I thought we were going to crash I wouldn't be on here either".

The flight was probably the roughest I'd ever experienced. It was a small plane and we were rocking all the way. I had a weird 'we're going to die' thought going on for the whole trip. This was very much out of character for me and the relief I felt when we stepped onto the tarmac in Canberra was overwhelming.

I knew that Mick's friend Doug was meeting us at the airport to chauffeur us around for a few days. We walked into the airport and there was Doug. I'd never met him before but something happened in that meeting. I've never ever been (and am still not) into esoteric fantasy. I'm not into using sexual energy to get attention. I had many connections of all kinds with all kinds of people, but this was something else. This was one of those connections that came from our energy and not from our heads.

Over the next few days we talked a bit and enjoyed each other's company. He expressed feeling the same strong connection that I was feeling, but Doug was married and I wasn't touching that with a barge pole. Peta and I flew out a few days later and I felt relief, actually, to be leaving and moving away from the strong connection that was there no matter what I did. I got back into work and that was that, or so I thought. The feeling kept creeping back in and I would push it away as fast as it came in.

One afternoon I was cleaning the pool. We stored the hoses for the vacuum on the roof of the shed for some obscure reason. I was up on the ladder grabbing the hoses to throw them down and the ladder fell backwards with me on it. It fell straight onto the edge of the pool. I couldn't move at all. I lay there for what seemed like a long time before Tim came out looking for me. He got an ambulance and I was taken to hospital. It turned out that I had done some damage to my back but the main harm was internal. My womb had come away from the abdominal wall.

I was released from hospital, but the consensus of opinion was that I needed a hysterectomy – and fast. I tried everything natural I could get my hands on to do it differently. I even tried resting (a very weird concept for me), but nothing was going to work. How do you get your womb to attach back naturally? I finally surrendered, went to hospital and had the operation.

Being fiercely independent, I drove myself, telling the kids to visit in a couple of days when I was stronger because I wanted to focus on my healing. Much to the disgust of my surgeon, I had homeopathics ready to start taking the minute I woke up. Anyhow, I was determined to take control as much as I could of my own health. Sounds funny writing that really, coming from someone who threw herself backwards off a roof.

During my stay in hospital Doug called me to say he was no longer a married man. What transpired with Doug was a relationship from different States that taught me *so* much about the enormous amount I was hiding the very vulnerable part of myself that needed to be a woman.

We spent as much time together as we could under the circumstances, learning from each other about reality in relationship. Doug was challenging for me, as he seemed to know when I was about to glaze over and do 'the running thing', albeit only energetically. He was very supportive and also very understanding when I needed to 'run away' for a while.

During my time with Doug, I realised that I'd found a friend who would assist me to work with things I'd been putting off for a long time under the guise of being a busy mother, alongside every other role I'd taken on board. All those wonderful childhood 'things' that keep us in our place, every small insecurity, came up during that relationship. I realised that's why I'd had such a reaction at the airport and whilst flying to Canberra that first time I met him. My energy knew what was coming. I was about to come face-to-face with some of my biggest issues.

As the relationship took steps towards becoming serious, I remember Doug saying one night, "Why don't we have a go at living together?" That was the beginning of the end for me. The reality of that relationship, the challenge of being pushed towards standing up and claiming my womanhood must have unconsciously terrified me and I did everything from that minute on to sabotage it.

Now let me state here that prior to that I had been in a marriage that would appear to the world then – and still would today – as the textbook 'happy family'. We did most things well. We loved our kids and worked together for their benefit. We weren't violent or abusive and in fact, when I look at the couples I now counsel, and even the ones I see out in the world, I realise we were very similar. We were just two people doing their utmost to work a relationship without many tools. We connected from the 'normal' connecting place that is enhanced somewhat by some sex and by having kids, but it's rarely a really deep and true intimate connection.

I know this now as clearly as I know anything else. The world connects from illusion a lot of the time. I connected with Doug from a very real place, that's why it scared me so much.

The upshot of this whole chapter, if you haven't pieced it together by now, is that having been faced with that kind of real and raw connection, without any thought involved I dived off a roof and created surgery that took away some female parts of my body.

I'm sure millions of people do things a lot more discretely than I do but I still believe they all create things to hide from real and raw connection.

19

Conditions

IN THIS CHAPTER I'D LIKE TO SHARE WITH YOU WHAT I'VE learned about the lengths we will go to as human beings, as men and women: to avoid, hide from and deny those parts of ourselves that lead us to vulnerability.

There are silent contracts we make at the beginning of relationships. Intimate relationships, friendships and all other kinds of relationships. These contracts are agreements we make in the energy to support a place we are comfortable living in.

For example, within a friendship one person

could be a saviour type and the other a victim type. So throughout the friendship these roles are played out continuously. If by chance one or the other learns about themself a little more and tries to change that relationship, the other person is going to react in a huge way.

Couples who are co-dependent (and I believe most are) have the silent agreement that things will stay as they are. When these things change for any reason the apple cart overturns.

In all of my experiences with people in my work, the common thread is that every person is yearning for a deeper connection with others. Whether it be with that one special person, or a more general feeling of just yearning for a deeper connection, even with themselves.

I have many clients who profess to have very intimate and vulnerable relationships with their partners, and then when I see them together, I am astounded at how little truth they tell each other. How often something comes up in counselling that they don't know about.

 Sex is not intimacy nor is it vulnerability. Sex is a function of the body. There are

times when the body needs sex and the feeling of it is not right or wrong. It just is.

The thing that makes sex the game it has become is the mind. Seduction has nothing to do with real connection or Love. It is based on manipulation.

I hear so often that couples, or one of the partners at least, regard having sex a certain number of times per week or month or whatever as an indication that the marriage is 'working'. Then of course if it doesn't happen the required number of times, the mind tells them that something is wrong. From there it is a downhill slide.

I know a vibrant young couple with two kids who live full lives and laugh about having sex maybe once every three months. When they do have sex it's incredible because their bodies need it and they do it for that reason. It connects them from that place and sustains their already close and intimate relationship. There is nothing in either of their minds that says there is a certain protocol they need to follow to be like the rest of the world. Sex does not make them good or bad or closer or not closer. It's just as it is and they love it and each other from a very deep and real place. Neither of these two people feel the need to prove anything to one another.

We've lost sight of something so rare and valuable. LOVE

If you have no respect, you have no Love.

What I have discovered both personally and in my work is that Love is living without guilt, without blame and without judgement, neediness or sadness.

In searching for Love, we are searching first for respect. Respect for ourselves and in turn respect for others. Once we respect ourselves at a deep level, Love becomes all about sharing ourselves and serving another.

When you have an abundance of Love springing from a safe place inside that has a strong and solid sense of self-love and acceptance of who you are, then there is no neediness. No manipulation or games are necessary. There is Love to share without conditions being placed upon it. With no fear of rejection or being left because the place inside you has no fear of being alone with yourself.

My recent learnings have shown me the possibilities open to all of us who are willing to take that next step away from fear and to walk that extra mile into those stronger connections. From here the dance of Love becomes a joy to behold. Sex becomes a beautiful dance. It becomes an expression of two people with deep and real self Love who can come together for a time and serve one another with every look and every touch.

It has nothing to do with manipulation or control. It has everything to do with the strength and truth of Love.

It's so far from the world we have created, where nobody stands in their truth and nobody owns their fifty per cent in relationships. The pulling and tugging of energy that goes on in nearly all relationships simply doesn't allow for the flow and expression of deep intimacy.

If you are having any opinions about how others need to run their lives – and that means your partner, your children, your work colleagues, in fact anybody – then you do not respect them. You do not respect that they can be in charge of their own lives.

Take the time I told my daughters to take care of their children around the water. It was totally out of line and totally disrespecting of the fact that they are capable human beings. I don't do that often, but the number of people who I see do it on a regular basis and call it helping is astounding.

A client often spoke to me about her daughters. As she spoke about one daughter her eyes would shine with pride. As she spoke about the other daughter there was a different energy. Perhaps it was pity. I know both of these girls, and they are beautiful and capable human beings. I know the mum thought that in her mind as well. But in her energy there was a 'lesser' factor running about the second daughter because she was a little overweight.

"A little", I said. So many times this 'concerned' mother conveyed stories about how disappointed she would be if the second daughter ate an extra potato at dinner. In fact, the whole family would frown in disapproval. The daughter did it anyway and would get angry about their disapproval. Her mum would explain to me that they were just trying to help her, as "she would feel better if she dropped some of that weight".

I believe the only people who would have felt better were the mum and the other family members. Why? Because then they would not be judged. They obviously believed that people were frowning upon this girl and in turn, upon them.

I'd like to say here that this girl is one of the most creative and talented girls I've come across. She is talented in so many areas of her life – much more talented than the rest of the family and she happened to be a size twelve.

There was very little 'said' about her weight. Which incidentally was absolutely perfect for her. The family were pencil thin and that seemed to be what they expected of her. The underground energy of 'not quite good enough' was loud and clear. She felt it and she reacted accordingly. She gained a little more weight, spent less time being active and lay around on the couch more often.

This story is very common. It is just one of many ways we 'disapprove' of something in someone else when it's actually none of our business.

So many people's lives do not reach their full potential because of others simply holding limiting thoughts or opinions about how it 'should' be.

It can be the opposite and just as limiting. Take for example, those thoughts about what our children should become – building kids into Princes and Princesses who believe the world owes them something because of their 'special' qualities.

All children have special qualities if we build that foundation I speak of. That solid place of Knowing who they are early on without our opinions and judgments. If we did that we would have children who were strong and solid and knew exactly what they were here for, what they were here to bring to the world.

The 'special' ones are equally as unable as the victims to find who they truly are. Just like those kids who feel 'less than', they are struggling to see daylight in a world where if you do not match up in some way you are no good.

The Princesses then start to compete and compete. Everything becomes chronic competition from which there is there is no way out. Eating disorders, depression, our climbing suicide rate all start and end with kids with no solid foundation. Kids who do not know their Place in the Boat.

We are building societies with people and communities who are trying to outdo one another. Trying to know more and be 'better than'.

Where is the connection from a real place? Where is the vulnerability? Where is the intimacy?

 Each of us has our own unique individual spark that is there to ignite our life. We all have that fire in the belly that can drive a life forward and no one else has that same unique spark.

Whilst writing this book there were a couple of times I felt I needed one of my team to just 'streamline' the wording. She is an awesome writer and her words flow very well. I sent some of the work to her and she streamlined it for me. When it came back I thought how wonderful the wording was and how she had explained things perhaps a little better than me but something didn't 'feel' right.

Of course it didn't, once we discussed it. That writing, as good as it was, did not have my unique spark, my energy behind it. It didn't sound like me. Once you find that place, everything fits and everything works.

If each individual understood, for example, whether their unique energy inside was male or female, then they would learn whole new ways of working and operating with others in the world.

What if some women had more of a male energy to work from yet tried to fit cleanly into a 'woman's role' in the world? And what if some men were energetically more comfortable being nurturers and supporters, rather than breadwinners and leaders? What if we all worked our natural instinctive roles rather than what society expects of us? Is it possible that there could be a lot more ease and flow to our lives? Would new possibilities open up for all of us if we weren't hindered by looking good and fitting in?

 We are so locked into the 'right' way to do things. Social consciousness is ruining our spontaneity and freedom to explore ourselves without judgement.

And that includes the freedom to allow our kids and teenagers to find out all there is to know about themselves by being allowed to feel and express their true feelings from an early age.

20

Death and Dying

I HAD A VERY WARM AND CLOSE RELATIONSHIP WITH MY NANNA. Ruby Florence was an amazing gutsy woman who had lived well and her stories about her tough beginnings kept us enthralled. She was a rock of Gibraltar when things were not great. Her passing was a special time. She was 94 and her body had simply worn out but she was feisty till the end.

Mum was amazing with Nanna. From the time she moved into the nursing home, Mum took care of her on a daily basis. When it was time for Nanna to leave we took her to a palliative care unit in Melbourne and I sat by her bed for the week or so before she died. In fact Mum and I took turns during the day with my brothers picking up the shifts during the evening.

My time with her in those last days was beautiful and precious. She was in and out of a coma but I read to her the books I had about God and angels and about the light – anything I could find that would give her peace.

One day I was reading a chapter about angels waiting for her when she left. She looked up at me with such fear in her soft grey eyes and asked me in a frightened voice, "Is any of that true?" I assured her it was my strong belief and that I was positive she would be welcomed. Her body visibly relaxed as I read more and more about passing gently and with Love. An hour or so later, after being in what seemed like a deep coma, she opened her eyes and looked at me. She held my hand and said, "Thank you." It touched my heart. It is a beautiful memory that I treasure.

As was the case in Nanna's life, she commanded an audience before her passing. Without abandoning her comatose state, she waited for my uncle and aunt to arrive from interstate, and also for her brother and his wife and my cousin. Mum and I were there of course, and from memory my brother, too. She waited.

And then once everyone had gathered she was gone in fifteen minutes. God love my Nanna Ruby.

I have been very blessed in my life to have worked with many people who are in the last weeks and days of their lives. If you have the courage to go there, there is a level of connection that can be made in those last days which can assist that person to let go of old wounds, help them connect back to family members where communication has failed for years and give them the opportunity to pass over with a gentleness that eases the pain for everybody.

A friend was dying of cancer. He was within a week or so of passing over and was feeling very panicky about so much. His family were an amazing support for him and gave me the privilege of assisting both him and them in his last weeks. I felt, and still feel very honoured that they trusted me with that role.

A week before he went to hospital for the last time, we were sitting together in his room at home and he expressed enormous fear and panic about his situation. His panic was almost out of control and his body was so weak and frail it was difficult for him to breathe.

He asked me if I could teach him to meditate. Knowing we didn't have a lot of time (and that it's no easy process to learn to meditate when you are in panic mode) I asked him to look outside his bedroom window where he lay, and look at the leaves on his beautiful gum tree. He did this, and as he did a light breeze picked up and the leaves rustled gently. He watched the tree for a really long time with tears in his eyes at the simplicity of that connection. How easy it had been for him to drop down to a place that was a little more real – still frightening maybe, but much more peaceful.

He had planted the tree years earlier and he loved his garden but he never thought to lie there and just watch the tree with all its' different aspects. I explained to him my belief about giving to Nature through taking care of the land and your garden, then being able to receive such gifts as this from the trees and plants, the sun and the wind when we needed to. Panic comes from the head. If there is any way to connect from your gut, from your heart rather than your head, panic will not be present.

We spoke honestly about his concerns in the last days and we were able to bring up lots of things that bothered him. There were many areas where he felt he wasn't able to find peace and we dealt with them. He spoke to his loved ones about his concerns on his deathbed and was able to pass over with most of his family around him, supportive and loving, allowing him to pass with Love.

I found myself in another situation one night that brought different challenges but the same result. I was with a couple of fourteen-year-olds boys and one of them had taken an overdose. Help was on its way but it was clear to me on arrival this boy was not going to make it. He was in the last stages of his life.

The boys' friend cried and said "sorry" a million times. They had never done drugs before and had decided since their parents were out it was a good time to give it a try. They had no idea about amounts, and this was the result.

My only thought at this point was about the boy that lay dying. The panic from the other people in the room had him in absolute terror. His eyes were wild as I approached. I ordered everyone out of the room in no uncertain terms, sat beside him and held his hand. His words were garbled but I could just make out, "Dad's going to be so angry with me. I didn't mean it. I'm going to die aren't I?"

I couldn't help this boy medically. All I could do was sit and hold his hand. The guidance that never lets me down and is always accurate if I'm in a real place, said loud and clear, "There is nothing for you to do but Love him now. Alleviate his fear and we will do the rest." All I knew how to do was try and connect with him from that sure place I had inside me and allow him the opportunity to try and reach that place in him where his Knowing came from. I spoke with him about believing that if he did die he would be taken care of and that angels would be waiting to take him home.

I told him I would speak to his parents and make sure they understood his fear of their disapproval. I managed to get him to understand that parents always loved their children even if they were mad at them. The fact is I don't believe anything I *said* to this boy helped him at all. It was what I *felt* that he was able to feel. From the true place inside me I could just simply Love him for the precious soul I knew he was. His panic subsided and he passed away fairly quickly.

The reason for telling this story is that I've seen a lot of people pass over without support. Fear has driven the circumstances and so many people die alone without the truth ever being spoken.

I mention it often in this book but it's a real passion of mine to speak out about that place of honesty inside us where our Knowing and our Love comes from. In that place there truthfully is no fear.

Over the years, I've learned the art of Tough Love, and going to that place is what it takes. Speaking to people in their last days about death when they don't want to hear it, challenging people when I feel the truth isn't being spoken, is not always easy.

There is often massive resistance and it would be easy to back away quietly and allow the opportunities to be missed. As a rule that's not my style, however, there are times when the Knowing is just as clear that these people are choosing to die and to do it without awareness. That's the only time I back away. Mostly, I can feel their need to know themselves strongly in the last days, even if they are weakened physically. For most people, the need to connect with some truth, particularly in the last hours, is strong. Therein lies another key to truth and gutsy communication.

These are times to take yourself completely out of the picture, step aside and be there completely for another human being. I hear time and time again that people are always giving and that they are always going out of their way to help others. It seems to me that 99.9% of 'giving' these days is giving with an attachment, which means that something is always coming back to the giver for their efforts.

I was privileged to be in a training once with an incredible Teacher. We had been asked to write a list of things we'd given unconditionally. I had a huge list. It was slashed down to one (with very good reason) and then I was shown how I really worked this particular claim to fame. Every day I'd walk my dog down to the local park. It was a stunning piece of natural bush and I loved being there. I connected to Nature there in a really profound way and my way of giving back to this land that was so beautiful was to clean up all the mess I found lying around. I never told anybody I did this, so figured it must be unconditional.

I was questioned about it and underneath my story of 'giving' was an underlying resentment about the fact that people had dropped the litter. It wasn't really a conscious thing, but once the energy was brought up I saw that it was absolutely correct. I was not giving unconditionally.

21

Back against the Wall

I WAS WORKING IN QUEENSLAND WHEN TIM CALLED TO SAY that his mate Scotty, a great family friend, had been sentenced to seven years in prison.

Scotty was a wonderful kid. He had spent a lot of time on our couch at home after going car racing or to parties with Tim and their other mates. Whilst travelling home one afternoon he lost control of his car on a corner and hit a motorbike. The guy on the bike was killed and his woman passenger was seriously injured. No alcohol or drugs were involved. It was an accident.

Now he was behind bars. Tim was devastated, so I could only begin to imagine how Scotty felt. As I sat looking at the ocean one day, asking for answers, it became crystal clear that this could be the beginning of a whole new life for this young man. I had clear information that this was the crossroads of a life that could be extraordinary. It was a choice point. A serious choice point albeit, but I received the message loud and clear. His life would most definitely go one of two ways now. I was asked to be the messenger.

"Right then." Scotty was a gorgeous kid and I loved him dearly. However, he was 'one of the boys', a racing driver. He was the one who would come out into the driveway of our home after a night out, look up at the beautiful birds crying out overhead and make comments like, "If only I had a gun", which horrified me.

How on earth do I now write him a letter, the day after he's had the shock of his life, to tell him I'm receiving clear guidance about passing on to him some pretty obscure things about the choices that were actually facing him now?

The things I was being told were not generalities. They were specific things I knew nothing about but that Scotty would certainly know. Having said that, I'm pretty sure that his mind would not be operating too rationally given the state of shock in which Scotty found himself. All he would know is that he was locked behind bars facing seven years in gaol. Even his lawyers had said there was no way he'd be locked up. It was one big shock to his entire family and his wide circle of friends.

I hesitantly wrote down what I was being told. I read it over and over again and couldn't shake the feeling that he was going to throw this back in my face. I got home later that week and handed the letter to Tim. He sat on the couch and read it several times with tears streaming down his face. Then, in his classic style he turned to me crying and said, "It's right 'Out There', Helen, one of your weirdest yet. But I know in my gut you have to send it". I posted it that night.

In Scotty's own words, "I received that letter and thought you'd gone completely mad". He was angry about it and put it aside. However, something inside him was stirring and he couldn't leave it alone. He told me he kept picking the letter up and reading it, then throwing it down again, as he just couldn't make sense of what I could be trying to get him to see.

Tim went to see him, spoke a few words and then let him talk. This young nineteen-year-old was facing the most major crossroads of his life so far. His head argued and yelled about how crazy I was to send the letter, but this wasn't about me. I had delivered something to him from something way outside of me, or of him, and he felt it.

He called me about a fortnight after he'd received the letter and asked for help. So the work began. I felt so blessed to be allowed to go to the gaol and work with this kid to help him get under all the 'man's world' reasons why he'd found himself behind bars. Blessed that I could help him step aside from the fear, which was immense in the beginning, and look at something so far-fetched for him that it made his head reel.

He was the most willing client I've ever worked with. Every week he was waiting for new things to try and new things to feel.

I shared insights with him about the way he'd lived his life so far that presented huge dichotomies, they were so different to what his mind had been telling him was true. He took them on and felt them, which wasn't easy for him to do at times but he did it. He worked with Nature. He got himself onto gardening patrol to help him give back to the earth and he encouraged others to do the same. He learned about his energy.

In a situation like that in prison, where a lot of the basic comforts of life are not there and your mind is telling you a million different things about *how* to feel, to be able to find a place that you can *feel* from instead of think for a while was a great comfort to him.

He found a sense of himself, a true sense that he'd never known before. Over a couple of years this young man took on concepts I find difficult to get through to people who've 'worked on themselves' for twenty years. He talked to me at times about how easy it would be to become part of the system and to just fall into the prison way of life. This of course is what happens for most people, and then on their release it becomes so difficult for them to break the cycle, particularly after such a long time. Scotty was extremely grateful for the opportunity to have an alternative way of doing his time inside.

It was difficult thing to really get a sense of what it was like to be locked up like that, and I pondered it often during my time working there. In the beginning there were moments when I'd be led through the gates and they'd slam shut behind me, or I'd be left in the medical centre, which is where I normally conducted the sessions, and there would be no guards there, only lots of guys waiting to see the doctor. Occasionally a question would cross my mind around how safe I actually was in those circumstances.

One morning I was working with Scotty and another guy in the library when a siren sounded. I had no idea what it meant but was told that we needed to go out into the yard as someone was missing and the guards would be doing a head count. This all sounded fine. We filed out into the yard with a hundred or so other guys from the prison. The gates were locked tight; the yard was in-between the library and the kitchen. As I looked around at these men, I realised that not only was I the only woman in the yard, I was the only civilian, so to speak. The guards had placed themselves outside the yard. There was a moment of panic and my mind ran a few very quick scenarios that did not impress me at all. If a riot started or someone decided to prove a point right now I was in deep trouble and by the time the guards had opened the gates and got in to stop anything, it could all be over. The men around me seemed like mountains. They were probably not all as huge as they looked that day, but the mind does funny things when you're in fear.

It occurred to me that I was completely out of control and out of my depth right now. I started to get a feeling, a very small one obviously, but a feeling nevertheless, of what it must be like to be locked in these circumstances for long periods of time. It gave me a new level of respect for the work Scotty and his mates were doing to stay strong and work on their Soul journeys under these conditions.

I looked outside the yard to the trees and the sky and asked God to help me. I really asked him, there was nothing esoteric about this. From my heart I said, *"I need you now God. Can you hear me?"* I must have been as pale as a ghost.

John, the other guy I had been working with, who is built like a tank and has a lot of influence with the men in gaol, walked up behind me, put his hand on my shoulder and said, "You're okay, nothing's going to happen while I'm here". I took the biggest breath I'd ever remembered taking. I must have been holding it for a while. After that, the hour or so we were 'locked down', was great. I mingled and got to know some more guys. It was interesting to hear their comments around seeing me arrive each week and wondering what I was doing, and they opened up fairly quickly about how they themselves were feeling in different ways.

After working with Scotty for some time weird things started happening on my journey to the gaol at Castlemaine. Two or three times my car broke down and I couldn't get there. Another time I got there and there had been some trouble so they wouldn't let me in. Things like that would happen, where I was left feeling like I'd let Scotty down in some way. We would speak about it on the phone and he was fine with it but I had this nagging feeling about it all. I finally realised, when something else happened during my next attempt to get there, that my time with him was complete. It was time for Scotty to do it on his own and open up into whatever was in store for him.

Scotty now runs groups in prison to assist others to find that unique place to work from. He's got himself a business degree, but mostly now he connects to others from a place he never knew existed. He rang me one evening overwhelmed, telling me he'd been involved in a working party group within the prison that day. A group of men were working to improve life in the prison for everyone. It was an ideas forum really, to see what was missing and how they could go about improving it. He told me that he'd been sitting facing some of the toughest men on earth, men with histories that would terrify even the most fearless.

When Scotty's turn to speak came around, the question being posed was that something was missing but they weren't quite sure what. Many guys had given Scotty their ideas but he said in that moment he felt something inside him that had to be spoken. He stood up and his head started to run. "Don't say it", or "Say something different. You can't say this to these men."

His courage prevailed. He spoke from his gut about how he felt that the one thing missing in the system that could change things was Love. He told me that as he spoke he was looking around the room and his head was running wild with all the possible scenarios that could unfold with him saying something so obscure. He said it anyway. The response, after the first initial stunned silence, was a nodding of heads and agreement from everyone in the room that it was the connection from the real place (which of course is simply Love), that was missing. Scotty will be leaving the system next year and is very excited about his amazing new life.

A choice point which is fully accepted and worked through, even in exceptionally tough circumstances, leads to extraordinary things.

A FOOTNOTE TO THIS CHAPTER:

I received a phone call from Scotty on Christmas Eve 2005. It was great to hear from him. He said "I'm ringing to let you know that my time is almost up. I'm being released in mid-January and I wanted you to know I'm looking forward to an exciting life. The choices I have made for a better life both in here and out in the world came from you working with me when I first came here. What you taught me has given me the strength to make those choices."

22

Stadium Story

MUM WAS ON A WELL-DESERVED MONTH'S HOLIDAY IN DARWIN. I had Katie while she was away and we were heading off to basketball for a night game. Katie was probably about eight at the time.

We were running a bit late, so I dropped her at the door of the stadium and went to park the car. There were no spaces in the front car park so I drove around to the back, which wasn't normal practice for me. It was pitch-black as I pulled into a parking spot a long way from the stadium. As I stopped the car my driver's door was wrenched open. There wasn't time to think. I was pulled from the car by my hair, thrown to the ground and then a man wearing a balaclava came down on top of me and started hitting me.

I went into survival and started fighting. He was strong and he held me down, speaking in a very quiet voice. He said "I am going to rape you". I looked up at this masked person then that familiar fight that started deep in my gut reared up and the thought was, *"Oh no you're not!"* I started to fight and scream. A car pulled into the car park and I thought to myself *"Help is on the way"*.

The people in the car obviously heard the screams, saw us on the ground and proceeded to walk inside to play squash. My mind was reeling, *"They're not helping, what do I do?"*

From somewhere I found the strength to take him on. I fought like never before. In fact, the final straw for him was I found his eyes and dug my fingers in as far as I could. He hit harder but he started to pull away. He got up and started running as a man from the stadium appeared to see what was happening. I shouted at him, "He's attacked me, go after him!" He turned and walked back inside.

I took off after him myself, but he got away. I had no idea what I was going to do but I was angry by now. I went inside and asked the man why he hadn't helped and he replied that he had gone to call the police. I am still stuck on this one. I can't imagine not chasing him down. My mind was saying, *"What if he goes after someone else now?"* However, that's me, and not everyone thinks like that.

Police and helicopters surrounded the area and searched for the man who had raped three women in surrounding areas at sporting facilities in the previous five weeks. Fortunately, no other women were raped in our area after the attack on me – I had a sneaky thought that hopefully he couldn't see them anymore! Also, as a result of that assault, the local council were driven to install huge spotlights in the car park at the rear of the stadium, which backs onto parkland.

The key to this story is really in what happened afterwards. The policeman escorted me home and stayed and interviewed me for some time. One of things I said to him astounded him and he reacted. He kept asking if I would be okay in the house alone with the kids. I assured him I would. During our conversation I said to him, "I'm glad it was me and not someone else". He was mortified. He couldn't understand why I had said that and I guess when I thought about it I wasn't sure either. My mind said, *"Thank God it wasn't a child or young woman that couldn't fight him off"*. That was logical to me. Today, I guess that thought came from my childhood, where I did my best to protect my siblings on many occasions believing I could handle it better than they could.

My Father was hitting my brother one night and I taunted him and hit him until he turned on me. My thought then was as it was the night at the stadium, *"At least he's leaving Peter alone"*.

We've lost the impulse to fight for what matters. Calling the police was enough for that man at the stadium – and it did have to be done. But it's a bit like giving money to charity instead of giving of yourself to another. There's a lot of looking good and keeping safe. We don't have to do anything more because we did the expected thing.

I've always been a fighter. In the beginning I learned to fight for survival. That evolved into a determination to fight for what really mattered to me in every moment ....now it's evolved into a fight for Tough Love on the planet.

Why does the world turn a blind eye? Because people fear they can't control the outcome? Because they fear for their own safety? Fear that they might be pulled into getting more involved than they want to and where would that lead?

Fear stops us from supporting a moment and it smothers a gut instinct.

There are situations where people might react quite cleanly in differing ways to each other, but when someone is screaming with terror something often stops us from banding together to go to their aid. What's *that* about? But then again, the exact same thing happens all the time in everyday life, take a situation like witnessing bullying in the schoolyard or workplace, or letting snide comments pass by at a dinner party.

It's a conspiracy of silence.

23

Choice Points

I WALKED TOWARDS THE HORSE PADDOCK AT THE REAR OF OUR property. It was a time I loved. Pa would often come and help me feed the horses at dusk. I'd give them their feed and sit there for a while just enjoying the peace.

TANGY AND NUGGET WERE OUR HORSES – Jo's and mine. They were one of those freedom things for us. The freedom that came from getting on our horses and going off on our own. We'd often ride up the bush track to the top of Mt Dandenong, which was close to home, and we'd sit on top of that mountain and look down over the city and surrounding areas.

This night, as I approached the horse paddock, I

felt a sense of fear. I knew something wasn't right, but as we do, I ignored it and kept going. I lifted my head from the feed bin and the next thing I knew I was opening my eyes to see my parents looking down on me, full-on panic stations all around, as I was being rushed inside the house to wait for the doctor.

Someone had apparently hit me over the head with a brick. They'd left the brick lying beside me and run. They didn't find out who did it, although I have a fairly strong sense it was a boy I had gone to school with. This boy and I had a long history of fighting with each other. A month earlier I'd received a phone call from the local butcher to tell me that Jo was being assaulted by him and three of his mates. I raced down there and physically took on all four of the boys, inflicting enough damage for the butcher to still be talking about it thirty years later... So maybe this was payback? Who knows? It doesn't really matter.

What an unfolding this book is for me. As I sit here and write I realise how many times I've been injured. I ask myself, *"Why? Why, over my life have I created being hit over the head or injured so many times?"* There has to be a huge learning in this for me.

I've sat with this for some time and my take on it is that each time it has happened, I have been close to feeling true, intimate connection. Not the sexual energy, not the 'man's world' love thing with its co-dependence and its manipulation of one another to stay safe. In fact not something that is familiar to me at any level. It's a connection that asks me to step up in some way. To give up some of the patterns I've developed, as we all do, to keep myself in the comfort zone. To keep myself in the safe place of giving when I feel like it and not giving when I don't feel like it.

It is something that obviously affects me in very profound ways. Profound enough to create incidents where I am literally taken out of those moments and placed into drama. The drama, I believe, created a smokescreen for the truth of what was happening in that moment. And it was often a drama big enough to take me away from that feeling for a long time, sometimes years.

I don't think this is unusual either. My stories are extreme – that's the way my life ran in those days. But I believe that we each have several pivotal choice points in our lives which are the catalysts for how we operate. And they are not always the obvious ones.

The statistics on depression today are staggering. My belief is that we don't have to take tragedy to depression. There is another way to deal with tough things. Depression, to me, mainly strikes when people hit something in their lives where they have a tough choice point and they hit fear. Fear of standing up. Fear of rocking the boat. Fear of facing change. That change can often be frightening, but only if they are not willing to feel inside themselves to *know* what is right. Once they hit the fear people often withdraw or withhold their energy from the world. They lock it down inside themselves and it creates that state of depression.

It's interesting to listen to people when they start the journey of looking at the truth of themselves. Usually, the first thing they hit is "I don't want to look at my marriage or relationship because that's really good. I just want to look at me."

In ninety per cent of cases, the fear in that statement is amazing. Right there is the cruncher for a lot of the world. It's not about giving up relationships. After all, they are an incredible learning ground for how we operate. It's simply about looking at the truth of co-dependence and how deep that runs. My standard comment here would be, "If you're not prepared to lay everything on the table you might just as well go home".

Everything is so intertwined. If you are 'fudging' in one area it's going to sift through into all the other areas. If you are a control freak, or a victim, you will play that out wherever you are in your life.

Some months ago a client of mine broke down

in tears after hitting a clear truth for him that he felt used by his wife and children to gain more possessions. He felt the 'give me, give me' mentality hugely, and it was affecting him deeply and the place inside that he hit was very real for him. The challenge? He loves his wife and family dearly, as they do him.

How can he say those things to them in a way that won't make them feel less or bad or guilty? How can he get across to them that these are just his feelings? He couldn't. The risk involved in saying these things was too great for him. He felt very strongly that he would lose his family if he spoke out.

Over the next few months this man went into the black hole of depression. He couldn't sleep and his work started dwindling away, which of course put him right into the place of feeling he was not a good provider, which in turn made the family panic that their 'wants' wouldn't be met. A vicious cycle that can lead nowhere other than to depression or apathy.

We went through several alternative ways that he could say what he had to say without offending. He couldn't muster the courage. The depression deepened. In this place there is no work for me to do – the work has to be accepted and undertaken by the client.

That's the thing about courage. It has to well up from inside a person. Noone else can do that for you. Otherwise it is based on someone else's beliefs and not your own. And that is not sustainable.

Finally he found the courage, spoke up and the depression lifted. I don't know whether or not the family received it well. The point is the truth was spoken. Once that is done, it is up to the individual how they deal with the outcome. Another person's reaction is actually none of your business.

24

The Kid

DURING MY RELATIONSHIP WITH DOUG I SPENT TIME GETTING to know his daughter, Bindi. She was a gorgeous, dark-haired teenager who loved her dad immensely, as he did her. Doug called her The Kid. He brought Bindi to stay with us occasionally. She was bright and easy to get along with. We talked a great deal and created a strong connection.

After the relationship ended, Doug and I stayed in contact from time to time, and during one of these contacts he expressed concern to me that Bin had started using some drugs. I spoke with her on the phone several times and it was obvious Bindi had decided to experiment with the new friends she had found.

Doug went the extra mile as a concerned and caring parent to help Bindi get through this time in her life. Without pushing too hard, we talked about how he could assist her and get through to her without making the situation worse. After a while it looked like Bindi was back on track. Doug told me that she'd moved back in with her mother and things were getting back to normal.

I hadn't heard from Doug for some time when, one afternoon, I walked outside and a white feather drifted down from the sky right into my hands. As it did, I had a strange sense, a Knowing maybe, that something wasn't quite right. I didn't think about Doug at that minute, but shortly after the phone rang and it was him.

He had found his baby girl, Bindi, under a bridge. She had died of a heroine overdose. Bindi was sixteen-years-old at the time of her death and the family now had enormous amounts to deal with.

Her mother had called Doug that afternoon to express concern that Bindi had not come home. He got in his car and started driving around. He had no idea where to look, but he tells how he heard Bindi asking him to go to the place where she was born. Doug's gut instinct did not like what it was feeling, but he followed the direction and drove towards the hospital where Bindi had been born. As he approached, he instinctively went to the bridge opposite the hospital, where he found Bindi.

The story that unfolded for Doug and the rest of his family during that time is tragic. Doug did his utmost to understand such a loss. He also did what he could at government levels to find out why this had happened and what could be done to stop this senseless waste of precious life.

I spoke with Doug recently. It's been ten years now since Bindi died and there are still questions he needs to ask. He expressed feeling good about his life now with his long-term partner whom he adores. But the questions still remain.

After Bindi's death I went to support Doug at the funeral. He was in a relationship with a woman at the time, but it seemed important for him that our connection was strong in his time of grief. It's not something that can be explained by either of us really. Just that I was there for him and he needed me to be. One of the most tragic things for me was speaking with a couple of Bindi's friends and hearing them describe her death as "the ultimate high". Good grief! What drives children and teenagers to that kind of searching? What is lacking in their lives that makes them strive for that kind of thrill? A thrill that ended the life of beautiful Belinda.

Over the next couple of years Doug would ring and I would listen. There was nothing I could say to him that would ease his pain, he simply needed someone to listen, without giving advice or holding judgment or telling stories of their own.

For me, supporting Doug was the most natural thing in the world to do, to a point. I was there to hold his hand at the funeral and there on the phone every time he needed someone to listen. He told me down the track that he had been offered counselling and also lots of advice from so called well-meaning people who tried to help. All he needed was to be heard.

I actually don't believe that all of those people are so well-meaning. I believe a lot of the time they are self-serving – 'filling their cup'. That's taking, not giving.

My friend Cass and I were there together for a few days around the time of the funeral. During the wake Doug stood with me for most of the time, holding my hand. Obviously he needed to do that and I was good with it for a while. Each time I walked away to talk to someone else he would look for me and call me back to stand with him. He needed support and I did my utmost to hang in there. At some point during the afternoon I felt the stirring in my stomach that told me it was time to go. Somewhere in the supporting, some of those old, 'other' feelings I had for Doug had re-surfaced. It seemed so easy and comfortable being there beside him. I made some excuse and left but in truth, I faced a fear that I couldn't handle and I made the whole thing about me.

I sat in the car and waited for Cass and some other friends. It was selfish and self-serving, but in true style Doug was onto it. He walked out to the car and leaned in through the window. He said, "I thought you were going?" I didn't answer and that look crossed his face, the one I knew so well. He smiled and said, "You've got those running shoes on again, haven't you?" It dropped me to the truth and I had to own that that's what had happened. He knew me too well and it scared me to death. Don't ask me why, it just did. He said he was leaving anyway and that he'd see me tomorrow. He wanted to meet me where he had found Bindi.

I'm great at supporting, but when it comes to receiving something back, accepting some energy that I have to take on myself, it's another story. I've worked on this a lot in the last few years. I didn't understand it at first, but it's become crystal clear now, and it's one of the main challenges I have to deal with.

As I drove away from that funeral I felt like I'd given enough. My head told me I would support him on the phone if he needed it, but I had to get home now. How's that? I'd given *enough!?* Never mind Doug, the father grieving for his beautiful daughter. It took one look from my friend Cass to tell me I was thinking about myself.

I went to meet Doug the next day. We spent some time under that bridge and he shared lots of grief. I am privileged that he did that.

I needed to get over myself and stop making it all about me.

Whatever it was that I felt, I know now that the need I have to run when I'm feeling pressured is garbage, and it's something I'm pleased to report is moving from my life.

25

The Turning Point

It had been a number of years since Jo died. We were growing and moving on through. I was working in welfare, attending university and bringing up all the kids. It was one of those times when you are feeling pretty good about yourself. I was achieving a lot, had my own home with the kids, Mum and Katie. I owned my car and was earning pretty good money.

But there it was, that stirring inside that told me something was missing. A friend had told me about a counsellor who worked not far from where I lived. Apparently, this guy was tough and had a new approach. I wanted to find out more. I made an appointment and went along to check him out.

Pete was good. He annoyed me, which was probably a good thing. But he called it like he saw it. He gave me some tips and sent me off with a book, 'The Way of the Peaceful Warrior' by Dan Millman. It's a brilliant book. I lay on my bed the next day and read it from cover to cover and it really moved me. It's a 'changing your life' kind of book.

I booked into a course Pete was running a few weeks later. It was a five-day retreat in country Victoria, to learn more about myself. From the moment I booked in, my energy was running. I was extremely nervous, which wasn't usual for me. I thought of every excuse in the book to pull out but something told me I had to be there.

I had to stop to throw-up many times on the way to that training. I'm not surprised now, because what they taught me was extraordinary. I was made to look at myself in a whole new light.

I had considered myself a good counsellor, however, these guys made me sit up and take notice of what my *energy* was doing. They took me on, which not many people did, in fact I remember throwing a book at Pete at one point in the middle of a group session and telling him where to go in no uncertain terms. I stormed out and sat outside for a while. Once I got out there I calmed down, got over it and went back into the next session. The judgment in the room from the rest of the participants was palatable. They obviously thought I'd stepped over the boundaries where the 'team' was concerned by calling him some choice names. I felt pretty isolated and I thought I was going to 'cop it' from Pete too, so I had my defences up pretty firmly. Funnily enough he turned it on the rest of the group and said I'd actually just expressed some energy and then got over it. It was they who were holding onto it. Now that was a new concept.

I don't remember a lot about those five days. They were great and I learned a lot, but I seemed to block out the details fairly well. I do remember being told I was running a lot of underground anger. I was told that I quite often shut people down mid-stream with my energy. I could cope with all of that, it was most likely all true.

Anyway, as I said, my life was looking pretty good on the outside and everything was running pretty smoothly. It was quite a shock to be challenged like this and to feel so much anger and resentment come up. It was also quite a shock that these people were 'onto it'. Being a counsellor myself, I was good at reading people and feeling what was going on under the surface. Now the tables were turned and someone was doing it to me. I knew most of the people I worked with in welfare were running a lot of their own stuff and using that as a basis for their counselling work, rather than working from a clean place, but I didn't think I was doing it. I was.

I came out of those five days with a thirst for more information about this underground energy. I continued to learn with the guys who ran that retreat. I got to know them and did a lot more work with them over the years.

One particular retreat I did brought about another level of understanding around the simplicity I need to work with. It was a spiritual workshop. I hadn't done a lot of that stuff but it felt right to give it a go. I had become very good friends with Pete, who had run the first workshop some years before, and he recommended the spiritual workshop highly. He told me it was very nurturing and that I'd have a wonderful time. Liar! I still love him dearly, but he lied vehemently. It was the toughest thing I'd done to date but I learned a huge amount and it proved a great tool for the gutsy communication work we now undertake in my company.

During this workshop we were asked to do a

guided visualization. It was a very powerful exercise and I felt a deep sense of what was happening. We were guided to 'lift up' and meet our Souls. It sounds a little weird and I wasn't really into all that stuff back then, but it was actually very beautiful. I allowed whatever was it was that needed to come up to surface.

It took some time for me to actually feel like I was having this meeting. My mind kept jumping in and telling me all kinds of things, like, "*This is crazy. How can it be real?*" But whatever happened during that visualization was profound for me.

We were asked to receive a gift from the person or Soul we had met and then come back to the group and share our experience. I listened as we went around and heard from everyone about their amazing experiences. People spoke of golden chalices filled to the brim and overflowing with love, treasures and jewels; some even spoke of deserted black lands with nothing on them but dust. As they were going around the group I thought about making something up. My experience seemed so small in comparison to their 'big' stories. I felt a little nervous about speaking up, but the fact is, my experience was my experience. When I met my Soul, I was offered a single daffodil. The voice I heard said, "When you work in the world, always keep it simple".

That simple message has been with me ever since. I realised, in hindsight, that the simplicity of what I do is the key to everything. There is so much information and analysis around these days that the truth gets lost.

 So when you see the daffodil appear throughout the pages of this book, my hope is that you will perhaps pause for a moment and feel the simplicity of this book and the story it has to tell.

As I've mentioned, over the years I did a lot of training with these guys. They taught me well. I learned all I could from them. I was blessed to be involved with them and since those days I have run workshops myself where Pete has taught with me. It was, and still is, an honour to have worked with them and shared friendships along the way. I think I've said before I'm an average friend. My life is so full of work that I neglect people at times. Pete was one of those people, but it never mattered. Each time we speak, even now, there's a sense of friendship and connection that nothing can take away.

A few years ago I undertook another year or so of training. During that time, myself and three other people were given the incredible gift of spending a few weekends being taught by the most amazing teacher I've ever had. During the last of these weekends I was aware I was receiving a level of training I'd never had before. I knew this was that big jump into the void that most people are terrified of and I was no different.

The weeks leading up to the trip were filled with outrageous bills which put me in a place of having to fight to find the money to go. There were also huge work commitments, I had a sick mother and then came the 'cruncher'. My daughter Niki, who was expecting her second child during the week of the training, went to the doctor to find that she had a thrombosis in her leg that was apparently dangerous. The doctor she and Damian went to see was new to the surgery and spent half an hour talking to them about the fact that if Niki experienced any pain or shortness of breath, she really needed to be rushed to hospital as she could very well die.

They came to my place straight from the doctor's surgery. This was the day before I was to travel interstate for the training. I watched my daughter sitting on my garage floor sobbing and asking me who would look after her babies if she suddenly died. She was frightened and I wasn't about to leave her. She was going to have to undergo massive doses of awful medication to contain the clot and the baby was about to be born. The birth became a whole lot more of a risk and the whole thing felt insurmountable as I watched her cuddling her two-year-old son, Toby.

I went into protection of my child, even though she was thirty, and I decided point-blank I would not go interstate to the training, just in case. What I was telling myself was that I knew she would be okay, but that I'd need to be there for Toby if she had to go to hospital. Then, of course, came all the justification. Really, it was taking a bit of a chance to go anyway, as her second child could be born while I was away. I totally ignored the fact that Damian's mum, Nanny Chris, was equally as capable of dealing with whatever came up for them as I was.

I spent a long time that night wrestling with something I didn't understand. If I got right down to the truth, I wanted to go. I knew I would learn something there that would change the way I operated in the world. I'd learned enormous amounts about the underground stuff and I was working with that to the best of my ability, but this was different. This was an extraordinary opportunity to gain wisdom from the incredible Teacher I mentioned earlier, the most profound I have ever encountered.

Still my daughter needed me. Although right here I have to say that Niki was saying all the way through this, "Go Mum, I'll be okay, and even if I'm not what can you do?"

But I wasn't going to be told... of course.

The next morning Niki had an appointment with her own doctor. He is one of those straight-up, straight-talking guys and I like him. I went along with her to see what he had to say. Prior to this, I had made phone calls to let people know I wouldn't be going to the workshop. It's weird, because as I write this, I know there was somewhere inside me that knew without a doubt I had to be there and that I would be. But it didn't make sense in my head so I let it go.

My old friend Gin, who was one of the four of us going to the training, called me just as I was about to go with Niki to see the doctor. I told her I wasn't going to the training and she said all the right things about being sad I couldn't make it and all the rest of it. Then as we were about to hang up she said to me, "Wheels (that's what they call me), you know what? This has nothing to do with your daughter. This is because you don't trust God enough". That sentence floored me. I knew then and there, whatever transpired that day, that she was right. Who did I think I was?

As Niki arrived to pick me up she looked at me

and said, "Mum, whatever happens here you need to go. I want you to go." Her doctor laughed at the dramatic way the other doctor had explained Niki's condition. Yes, it was fairly serious and she underwent all those horrible injections for a few months, but he looked at me and said, "Get to that training, mother. I'll take care of her and if her baby comes I'll do that too. That's my job". So I flew out that morning for what was the most profound experience I've ever had.

There are a couple of footnotes I need to include before I go on. Firstly, 'Wheels' is the name I was given at the first training I attended with Pete and his team. Hell on Wheels. Yes, I was a bit of a nightmare in those days and fought them tooth and nail. It didn't last long but I always had to start off fighting. The other thing is that my second beautiful grandson, Heath, was born the morning after I returned from interstate. Funny that – everything is as it's meant to be.

During my time at the training I listened intently and tried to stay open to everything we were being told. I have to say now, two and a half years later, I didn't really understand a lot of it. My head said, *"Yes, I understand"*; but truthfully, I wasn't ready to take on that level of work until a lot later. My mind heard it all but my energy still had to go through the entire process. Which is still happening today. It's a lot clearer now but I know I'm learning from that training everyday.

 It's funny how we humans hate being exposed, and what we will create to hide from it.

I have to say I'm a lot better with that than when I first started but the deeper levels can be covered up for a very long time, sometimes forever. That is unless you are truly committed to getting to the core of who you are and what you are here to do.

26

Reality versus Illusion

THE MOST VALUABLE LESSON I LEARNED IN MY TRAINING WITH Pete and the others was just how much goes on underneath what we say and often, even under what we *think* we feel.

We are impacting on people every minute of every day without even knowing it. In my company, we do a lot of work in seminars these days about the illusions that the world runs, about how people operate to stay safe. It's not a bad thing, just something we are not aware of. Once we become aware of it the world can open up into a whole new exciting realm, but it takes a bit of courage to have a peek.

It's always interesting when I hear about a wonderful, kind person who is doing so much in the community to help others. People admire them and look up to them. Sometimes what is claimed is the absolute truth and sometimes not. I have encountered many of these people who are in it for the applause, for the pat on the back, and if that's not forthcoming then there's trouble in the camp. It ends up being a way for these people to 'fill their own cup'.

Yes, of course I have a couple of particular people in mind but there's no need for names. To me, these people feel isolated and quite sad. They are playing such a game they've forgotten about reality. Their energy doesn't lie and their energy has underground anger running rampant. Our energy never lies. It's our egos and our stories that lie. On the other side of those lies, even though you have to walk through the mud to get there, is such freedom it's indescribable. And by the way, getting through the mud is not that tough. It's only our minds that make it tough.

If you feel deep inside, or even stop long enough to consider these things you will feel the stirring. If you have ever heard the call of the black cockatoo and felt a stirring deep inside, legend has it that this is the calling of your Soul to be recognised and awakened.

There are a few common themes that seem to run within our behaviour. We have fun with people at workshops playing with these themes and watching how people 'buck' at being told how they impact on others. There are lots of laughs, and lots of clear examples during the workshops, that show people how their behaviour plays out in the world.

We do have lots of fun with it. However, if people really take on the full impact of what's being offered it shows up how destructive the behaviour can be and how limiting it is in their life and in the lives of others.

You can tell me until the cows come home that there's a soft easy way to do this Soul journey. I can tell you with everything that I am…

you have to go through to get to the other side.

You may choose to stay on the same side and live an unfulfilled half-life, or even an average life, but if you want it all, if you want the guts and the glory, the passion and the pain – you have to go through to the other side.

It's in the fight that you find your courage and your tenacity. It's in the fight that you learn who you are and what you will actually fight for. Most people fight from their ego and fight to hold onto the Picket Fences and the illusions. That's why there are frustrated angry people all around us. And the living dead. Because the other killer is apathy: "It's all too hard so we won't look".

The esoteric/self help/New Age movements have brought us thus far with lots of good techniques and some great books with which to fill our libraries. Not only books but meditations, visualizations and a greater all-round awareness that there's something out there somewhere that we're meant to be connected to.

The downside of all this is that I believe the pendulum has swung too far. An imaginary gap has been created between those who 'know' and those who don't.

Take the churches or any other institution that claim they are the ones connected to God. You can go and be special with them as long as you do as you're told. Same with the New Age movement – there are the ones who 'know', then there are the ones who don't.

The ones who apparently 'don't', always look to others for their answers. The gorgeous Guru's, who are wildly filling their cups from the ones who 'don't', will espouse information until the cows come home.

The trouble is, I believe, the ones who 'don't' will never stand up in their own reality if they are continually put into second place by people who think they are in first place – by those who apparently 'do'.

How much easier would it get if each and every one of us were to actually find our own wisdom and work from that?

27

Wolves

SEVERAL YEARS AGO I WAS INVOLVED WITH DELFIN INTERNATIONAL, an American based personal development company. Leslie and Sandra Fieger headed up the company and were the writers and presenters for much of the material Delfin delivered to the world.

Those years were a wonderful training ground for me to step up into working with an international company where many of the conference calls I was involved in were worldwide. It was an opportunity to speak to people all over the world and to learn and grow alongside fellow travellers. The Delfin Knowledge System was a great program and the seminars were powerful events.

A year or so into my association with Delfin, Sandra invited me to attend the Seminar Facilitator Training on the Gold Coast in Queensland. I had no hesitation in putting myself forward as I'd had the privilege of meeting Sandra and Leslie when they travelled in Australia and knew in my heart this would be a training from which I would learn a great deal.

As is probably obvious by now, I often make it hard for myself to get to these big stepping stones. Although I had chronic back pain I got to the Gold Coast but then almost didn't make it to the training. I was sharing a hotel room with a woman I had met through Delfin and we aligned beautifully to sabotage one another's progress to the point where we called the organiser on the morning of the training and told him we wouldn't be attending.

Sitting on the beach that morning my gut sense started stirring. That voice was saying, "What are you doing? You have to be there". It was a quick taxi ride, and a few phone calls later we finally arrived just as the training was starting. And what a training it was! Sandra put us through hoops for three days. It was tough, challenging and I muddled my way through it. Every move we made was being filmed. Here I was on stage doing things I was not comfortable doing, with chronic back pain and, to top it all when I sat down, I had to sit on a huge rubber exercise ball!

Basically the purpose of this training was to find someone capable of facilitating the very large Delfin Seminars in Australia. I was a good counsellor and ran a lot of groups – sometimes reasonably large groups – but this kind of seminar was very different from what I'd done previously and here I was sitting on a rubber ball!

Some of the international participants were very slick operators. They had all the moves, they knew the stuff well. The way I work is I speak from my heart, as much as I know how to. I don't get into 'the moves' or the right way to do things. All that does is confuse me. I know that if what I'm teaching is based on the truth, as I know it, I never need notes and I never have to worry about being caught out or caught short in any way.

We were taken through gruelling exercises. Like telling our life story on stage and being filmed doing it. By this stage I'd already looked around the room and sussed out the competition. I figured I didn't have a chance in hell of taking out the honour of facilitating a Delfin Seminar so I might as well just put myself in fully and get what I could from the learning.

So I blubbered my way through the things I was stuck with in my life – on camera. And I did my best to absorb what I was being taught. My roommate was very slick. She ran lots of groups in her hometown and did a lot of other things in the world and her presentation was immaculate. In my eyes it appeared close to perfect.

The morning after the training, when the phone call came through to us and I was asked to facilitate the seminar with Michael Koren the next week, I was so stunned I couldn't speak. That was the beginning of an amazing learning for me.

I went up to the Sunshine Coast with my roommate and spent a few days on the beach figuring out what I would present at the seminar. It was going to be a full house and I was pretty nervous.

I've called this chapter 'Wolves' after a wonderful Garth Brooks song by that name. It moves me every time I hear it. The truth is, everything I came up with to present at the seminar was pulled down by my roommate. I had several good stories that had a humorous edge, and also some great lessons relating to those chapters from the Delfin System that I was to work with. Each one was criticized and put down very quickly – quickly but nicely, of course.

The end result was the one of the most debilitating feelings I've ever had. I had the job of doing the facilitation yet I couldn't find a place inside me that felt like I could actually get up and do it. I picked up the phone several times to call Sandra Fieger and tell her she'd made a mistake in choosing me. I didn't make those calls. I don't think I even had the courage to do that.

I struggled with not having the right 'material' for days. I didn't sleep; I paced the floor at night worrying that I'd be letting Sandra down if I didn't 'get it right'. Unfortunately, I kept sharing my concerns with my roommate as the nightmare built. I didn't have the right clothes to wear. People paying that much money for a seminar expected professionalism.

I have no ill feeling for my roommate at all. This is what people do to each other in this world. This is how I see people operate every day in my counselling practice with their partners, their kids, their co-workers. Not only in my counselling practice but in the world in general. It's all done in the name of helping and love.

I want to convey to you how it feels to be on the receiving end of this kind of energy – the truth of it's' impact. Without blame or judgment, just the truth of how it feels and what it's like to come out the other side.

The way it works in the world is sneaky. If someone comes at me with anger I can handle that really well. I had a great training ground when I was young, so I can meet that anger without fear and I don't feel at all threatened. The thing I couldn't handle back then was seduction. The seduction that is rampant in our society. We call it the Smiling Assassin syndrome in the workshops I run.

You know them. They're the kind who smile at you and tell you up-front that they are very sensitive. That's usually the forerunner for, "I'm about to slap you all around energetically. I promise I will always keep the smile on my face so no one can say I'm being mean but I'm going to push you down onto the ground and stand on your head.....with love.....and remember you can't yell at me because I'm sensitive and I'll probably cry."

These are the Wolves.

The technique worked on me a lot in the past. Trouble was, I couldn't see it coming. By the time I woke up to it I was already feeling terrible and it's hard to fight your way out from there. I always did eventually, but there could be weeks of doubting myself in between. 'Advice with an agenda' is what I call it. It's a daily practice for millions and millions of people and it's damaging. Nowadays I see it coming. I can almost smell it and I'm onto it immediately. Life's a lot easier.

Back to the Delfin seminar. I went for a swim the afternoon before I left the Sunshine Coast. I'm a very strong swimmer and was a lifesaver for many years in Melbourne. This particular afternoon I got caught in an undertow and for a few minutes I was in real trouble. As I was leaving the water after quite a shake-up I heard that voice in my head telling me very loudly, "You are being pulled down". I said "Yes, that was very obvious, thanks for that".

"You are being pulled down". I walked out of the water to my roommate who was anxiously asking me what happened. I looked at her and finally got what my guidance was telling me (in those days I heard the guidance loud and clear but second-guessed lots of things).

By the time I got back to the Gold Coast to stand up in front of all those people I was a mess. Of course I wasn't showing that to anyone, but inside I was in victim valley. It's a funny thing with me though, because although my head had me in that place, something deep down inside me knew I could do it. The head is a weird instrument. If we didn't rely on it and believe its' rubbish, we would be extraordinary beings.

The big day came. I was hovering outside the doors while the packed house sat inside, listening to the other presenters. I wasn't quite sure how to put one foot in front of the other to get through the doors and walk up on stage.

Let me explain something here. Delfin Seminars are 'the full shebang': lights, cameras, powerful loud music, huge screens playing amazing footage as you walk up the aisle to the front stage, and over a hundred people hanging off every word you are about to say.

That was the next thing. *"What am I going to say?"* This was getting decidedly worse. I walked through into the Facilitator Room at the back and Sandra was there, calm as always. I tried to be nonchalant and she asked how I was. I said I was fine but my insides were turning upside-down and inside-out.

I went back outside and Paul Niederer happened to be standing outside the door. He was the guy who had filmed the entire Facilitator Training so he had a bit of dirt on me, so to speak. He grabbed my hand and looked at me. He said, "You're going to do fine." I replied, "I'm a bit nervous." His response moved me to another place. He said, "If we all had a bit of what you've got – that honesty – then the world would be a better place." As he said it, the music started for me to enter the room. I stood at the side of the curtain ready to walk out, looked out at the crowd and froze again. My only thought was, "*I can't go out there, I've got nothing of value to say.*"

A voice in my head – so loud – said to me, "This is not about you. This is about what you can give to these people." Two angels in ten minutes. I walked out there proud to be part of this wonderful organization and proud to give my small part to these people.

The Delfin Experience moved me to a greater level of learning and allowed me to experience a part of me I didn't know existed. And Sandra was an incredible mentor for me. While presenting at my second seminar I was criticized by one person for a thing they didn't agree with and I felt okay until I got home, at which point the doubts crept in. I dreamed that night that Sandra walked into my room and said, "Get over it, get off your butt and get out there and do it. Own that stage and do what you know." It inspired me and since then I have facilitated further Delfin Seminars and enjoyed the experience immensely. I work with what I feel comfortable with and that's all I can ever do. I am honest, I love to have fun with people and it works.

So the other part of this chapter is the learning about the Wolves. I don't believe people want to take each other down, but they do. In my practice and everyday in the world I see the results of competition. The results of people's unconscious choices to try and prevail over others that are destructive in so many ways.

I could take this to the global context here and tell you how I think this affects the entire planet, however, this book is about learning to look at ourselves. Myself included. It's only the starting point to bigger places.

These small put-downs can be so insidious; as was the case with my roommate. My mind said she was assisting me but my heart knew differently. Let me reiterate that there is nothing bad about this, only that my friend had a perception that her performance could not help but be noticed and accepted as the best. When it wasn't, it was outside her reality and the only way her ego knew how to cope was to put me down to a level where I couldn't succeed either. Then we'd be the same again. I'm sure she would have consoled me very well and been my buddy but the damage had been done.

We humans carry out this energetic bashing for all kinds of reasons. I see people doing it with their kids – kids that they adore. It would never ever occur to them that their energy keeps their kids just a little smaller, just a little less likely to take risks, so that as parents they can stay safe and in control. It would never occur to them that it is actually damaging to that child's ability to simply fly. It is damaging to that child's ability to find his or her own way in the world with strong boundaries but with the freedom within them to flow.

Instead we build the Picket Fences. Now there's a topic.

28

The Picket Fence

THROUGHOUT THIS BOOK I'VE MENTIONED THE PICKET FENCE many times. I believe it's one of those things that keep us from being completely who we are. I talked about young Smithy back in our childhood, who was horrified about how we lived as kids but that what we felt in his house was somehow just as horrifying to us.

It's just different sides of the coin – what we become comfortable with. The trouble is living comfortably doesn't always serve us, and we usually don't know how to break the cycle. It feels like the world lives in 'comfortable', even though, mostly, it's not.

There are so many degrees of comfort. It's usually only the people we look at and see as the 'don't have's' that we deem to be 'uncomfortable'. The amazing thing is they may well be a lot more comfortable than the 'do have's'.

The numbness that being 'comfortable' creates is causing a blanket effect of apathy, depression and disease throughout society.

To get through this we have to expose – or have exposed – those things in us that keep us in those comfort zones. Yet exposure is one of the greatest fears lurking beneath every pattern and every stubborn resistance we have. My old friend Pete would say, "What if? What if you looked at it a different way and it changed your entire life?"

In the pages of this book, I've also talked about the Knowing which can be awakened with some elbow grease and lots of determination. I guess right now, if I feel instead of think, the Picket Fence is the very thing that keeps us from our Knowing. Most of the planet create and live in this illusion I call the Picket Fence. This place is not sustainable – it's the place that all the above stems from.

What is built inside these Picket Fences is a fortress, not the freedom we are yearning to attain. The freedom comes from the Knowing, the true Knowing without all the attachments, without the mind running its' games and patterns. As I've described many times, it's a place that you may not particularly agree with all of the time, but when the Knowing comes there is absolutely no denying it.

From here you have to be tough about your boundaries. You have to mind your own business a lot of the time, speak up when the energy is there to do so and shut up when it's not. You have to ward off the things that drain your resources and put the boundary firmly in place, which is often not a *comfortable* thing to do.

It means exactly the opposite to living inside the Picket Fence. Inside the fence, people create stories to keep the palings firmly in place:

"We really do love each other, we just don't show it anymore".

"We don't talk much, but that's okay because we have good sex occasionally and that keeps us close".

"We have to stay together for the children".

"We have to stay together because he or she is my soul mate".

"My parents stayed together and would be mortified if we separated".

"There's a lot of people worse off than we are".

"If I just hang in here he or she will eventually change. Or I guess we'll just get too old to care".

"We do lots of things as a family".

"I couldn't be bothered doing the dating thing again".

"He's better than so-and-so's husband".

"He doesn't spend much time with the kids but he's a really good provider".

"I couldn't face my children if I broke up the marriage".

And that's just the marriage side of things. The other relationship Picket Fences are equally as strong:

"I am not meant to have relationships".

"I had some bad stuff happen and I don't trust anymore".

"I am alone and aloof because I am on my spiritual journey".

"I couldn't do my soul journey and manage a relationship at the same time".

"I'm looking for the perfect partner"
And in other areas of life:
"If I please people all the time and they like me, then
 everything's okay"
"If I do as I'm told at work and don't rock the boat then
 I'll stay safe".
"I can't leave this job I hate because I might not get
 another one."
"If I work hard and get lots of money I'll be happy."
"I've got life worked out. If I accept I don't know every-
 thing then I'll be out of control and vulnerable."
"I control people because I really do know what's best
for them."
"People don't control me – they look after me and mean
well and I'd hate to hurt their feelings."

We work to create situations that look the way
they are 'supposed' to look – the way society, our parents, the latest self-help book, our religious leaders,
our partners say they should look.

The thing about Picket Fences is they can be
badly rattled by a serious challenge. On some level,
most people know this, because serious challenges are
avoided at all costs. Somewhere deep inside (although
often not consciously), most people know their Picket
Fences have been built on illusions. Shake the tree too

much and you might get hit on the head by a falling piece of reality. So the choice is made to 'keep things nice' because otherwise, everything we have created will be jeopardized. We might end up being impaled on our own picket fence.

But in the meantime, we are living strangled lives, we are working so diligently to maintain the status quo that we don't really give ourselves a chance to breathe. All we allow ourselves is the picture-perfect postcard that says, "Having fun, wish you were here". We don't give ourselves the chance to write the deeper story of our lives and we deny ourselves the freedom to truly live.

That freedom is available to everyone, but it takes work to find it. It requires the courage to knock down the Picket Fence and expose the illusions that have been holding it up. The ground you have been confidently walking on may start shaking as you start to feel the lies you have built your life on and the ways you have been denying your Knowing. Pretty soon you'll start to see the irony of fighting to keep a fence intact that has been built to protect something that isn't even real. You'll start to wonder why we build these fences to protect and contain our picture-perfect lives when all it ends up doing is robbing us of our freedom. But believe it or not, this is a good thing. It means you are getting closer to the truth, closer to the reality of your life and how you really feel about it.

Getting honest and real with yourself puts you in the best place possible to build an honest and real life. There is no more denying how you really feel, no more Picket Fence because you won't need one. You will be creating a life that feels strong and unshakeable because it's grounded in the truth. From here, you can get to know the things that really matter to you and build a life around those things instead of around fantasies that only end up hemming you in and stifling your chance to be truly fulfilled.

It takes guts to roll up your sleeves and dismantle your Picket Fence but the rewards are tangible and long-lasting. It also takes vigilance to maintain your boundaries once you are living in this new, real place because with freedom comes responsibility. Staying tuned into your feelings and true to yourself in the face of challenges from the outside is not always easy. You will find that your own ego will come up with all sorts of excuses to challenge you to keep your head down and get back inside that fence to stay 'safe'.

But the longer you live in this real and free place, the less you will feel the need to insulate yourself in a numbed-out comfort zone hidden behind a little Picket Fence. You will have no desire to go back to living a life that is so small that it could fit onto the back of a picture postcard. You will have opened up a whole new way of living and connecting to your-self and those around you by listening to your heart and having the guts to take the road it's leading you down.

 There's a strong energetic boundary that can be created around you from where your Knowing and the truth can spring. You have to work at this. You have to be willing to put yourself on the line for your dream.

Most people don't even know what their dream is – their Soul's dream, that is. That's because they live in the Picket Fence and can't see beyond it.

29

Shazz and the Duck

MY PERSONAL ASSISTANTS ARE SITTING BESIDE ME ALL THE way through the writing of this book and we've been working on how to get through the stories of the New Age movement.

The best way is personal truth for them so here it is.

Both of these women were heavily into the New Age/esoteric movement when I met them. Shazz was a practitioner/healer. Duck was a corporate genius with an overlay of her special connection to Spirit. Meditation and talking to angels were part of their daily routines. They had it all down to a fine art. They had their stories straight. Both of them had great lives with lots of everything they needed. It stands to reason that with these kinds of connections to Spirit, there would be a warmth, a loving side to them that was beautiful.

I couldn't find it. To me they were sad, isolated, lonely, aloof women who didn't connect to any kind of love. As they sat in the first group with me, I wondered how on earth I could connect them back to themselves and out of their absolute illusion and fantasy.

These are their stories.

SHAZZ

'When I first came to see Helen I had hit a place where I felt like a fraud – it was a long time coming and had been hidden beneath a very comfortable looking life. I had been searching all my adult life. I had read everything I could get my hands on, attended as many workshops as I could, held accredited qualifications in several alternative modalities and believed I had a duty to share all I knew. I also had what I believed to be a strong and clear intuition that assisted me to help others when conventional avenues ran dry.

It was some time before I understood that all the learning, the reading, and the studying was a distraction to avoid facing the fact that I really wasn't able to connect with people from a real and loving place. It looked like I did, and at the time I believed I did, however, what became clear when I was taken to a deeper understanding of how I operated was that I hadn't experienced the difference in feeling a real connection with another human being. I was operating from my head, not my heart.

My friends and family knew me as one of those people that others confided in. I was a good listener and appeared caring. Sure, I was listening intently, but just long enough to find the place in the conversation where I could jump in and show them what I knew in order to mend or fix them. I was holding myself up as the authority on how they should live.

I was considered a thoughtful and attentive practitioner; however, I was really preventing my clients from feeling their own Knowing by espousing my insights as if I were somehow more connected to their truth than they were. I wasn't even connected to my own truth, so how could that be?

I told myself and my clients that I absolutely believed that their healing came from inside of themselves. However, I took on the responsibility to deliver it to them. I was in the way of their own real connection to self.

Behind the scenes I felt something wasn't right, but I didn't understand why. I had enough evidence to prove to myself that I had read and studied enough. My clients were telling me all the right things so that I could convince myself I was doing okay. I had all the theories but I felt like a failure. Instead of doing something about that underlying struggle I buried that uncomfortable feeling. I studied harder, gathered more information, and lifted myself higher above the crowd – isolated myself more and more, so that I wasn't exposed, even to myself. I was exhausted trying to maintain my profile. I didn't let people in. I made sure I was self-reliant, not needing anyone. I apparently didn't have the same needs as others. No one was able to give or do for me. I would always know what I needed. My independence masked my arrogance and beneath that my insecurity was building.

I attempted to reassure myself I was okay by gathering people and crowds. I was known as the social events organiser. I told these people what they wanted to hear, slipping in as much advice as I could under the guise of helping. I gathered people who fed back to me what I wanted to hear. I did this at dinner parties, at workshops and at large gatherings. It was all about me gathering people to listen to me, sharing my imagined wisdom.

I didn't attract people who challenged me. I gathered people who supported the charade. I got my learning from school, books or TV. Places where I wouldn't be challenged. I fooled myself that I knew more so I didn't have to learn from others. This was never a conscious thought but it was running underneath all of my behaviours. Having the apparent psychic connection up my sleeve meant I could always console myself with words of apparent wisdom from a source others couldn't dispute.

Then I met Helen, who called it like it was. She was up-front, open and honest. She said that she wouldn't bother working with me as it seemed like I thought I knew it all anyway. That my attempts to know one better the whole time drove her nuts. My suggestions were full of self-righteous crap that kept me safe. I thought I was just helping people. People had always looked up to me and said I was friendly and thoughtful. Of course they did – they were the people I encouraged to be in my life, people I kept that 'one-up' thing running with so I would always be in charge.

I didn't want to hear what Helen had to say, but she'd got me. She also told me I felt lonely, sad and isolated. What the ****!! I didn't recognise that either. I was so ignorant of who I was. So that was what that restless yearning was about! Helen was onto me... thank God! Finally, here was someone who was prepared to challenge me for my own sake. Someone who was prepared to see past my behaviour, to feel the real me longing to connect with people. Someone who let me feel safe enough to actually feel the truth of who I was in my heart, not my head.

The work began with Helen and I have to tell you I am a really different person these days. I feel real. I feel honest. I used to think I was a crusader of truth before. That's just funny now. As if I could possibly know what everybody else's truth was! I was so determined to impress my will upon others, so worried about being right or looking good that I only shared things that would support my ego. I didn't do anger and whilst I loved to laugh at others I cringed if someone should laugh at me. I so needed to get off my high horse and get over myself. I am a work in progress. The freedom of not having to know more or to validate who I am is bloody marvellous.'

DUCK

'I was a thirty-five-year-old wife, mother and profes-
sional businesswoman. Working hard at keeping the
Picket Fence in position and being all things to all people. My head was telling me I was lucky to be where I
was and I was keeping up appearances pretty well, but
inside I was an exhausted, disillusioned shell.

At one point, I clearly remember saying to myself *'Is this all there is?'* A week later I found myself in
a meditation group for the first time, doing creative
visualizations which opened up a whole new world
within me. It was a place without confrontation, without fear and without the mundane nitty-gritty of everyday life. In this place I believed I could find peace,
be comforted by angels and start to create the life of
my dreams. Thus began the next seven or eight years
of intense personal and spiritual 'development'. I did
course after course and workshop after workshop. I
consulted clairvoyants and psychics on a regular basis
and I got to feel pretty good about myself and my loving connection to the universe.

Somewhere in the background my life went on.
The money came in, the kids grew older and the prob-
lems in my marriage intensified to a point where it
collapsed and ended. Even that was somehow okay

because I felt like I was apparently living on a 'higher plane,' that it was all meant to be and that somehow this so-called 'connection' with Spirit was carrying me through.

It was around this point that I met Helen and she started to reveal the truth of my huge illusion. I was fascinated by her passionate, humorous, down-to-earth approach to life. She showed me that a true spiritual connection can only be experienced by grabbing life with both hands and living every moment of it. Here was someone I could learn from. Granted, initially, I didn't believe she had a lot to teach me because I believed I was doing very nicely thank you. Nevertheless, somewhere inside I knew I wasn't. That what was missing was actually my life.

I began to feel the enormity of the extent to which I had numbed myself out, how I had used the pretence of spiritual connection and all my esoteric learnings to keep myself away from truly connecting with anyone. I had somehow managed to kid myself that I had love and compassion in boundless quantities but had ended up going through a marriage breakdown without an ounce of either. In fact, I've only recently felt a new level of the truth of what happened around that time, which was that I had become such an ice-maiden I had no place left from which to connect with the feelings of my partner, my children or myself during the most traumatic time of all our lives.

I know that thanks to Helen, I'd deal with it differently now. As she says 'shit happens.' I don't waste time any more visualizing, affirming and shielding myself from the emotional reality of life's inevitable ups and downs, and I don't beat myself up or reach for the stars when things do go wrong. Because I've got my feet so much more firmly planted on the ground, I'm finding there's more richness to life than I've ever experienced. And I laugh a lot.'

30

The Relentless Power of the Ego

I'VE HEARD MANY TIMES THAT WE NEED TO HAVE EGO TO SURVIVE. Well, maybe we need it to survive, but we certainly don't need the kind of ego that runs this world today in order to live. It's destructive, it's damaging and it prevents us in any situation from feeling the truth of who we are.

I have spoken about Princesses in this book. The kids who are held on a pedestal, where the parents run their energy through their kids in order to have some kind of life. These kids and teenagers have been put into a position where someone else's life is lived through them, where these kids 'making it' or not becomes the focus of the entire family.

It's wonderful to have goals and ambitions and to set those goals firmly in place and know what you are heading for. Along the way though, there needs to be room to grow and change.

For example I witnessed a guy who had clear strong goals to make a certain amount of money, be at the top of his company in a short time, make a success of his marriage and be a wonderful father. He achieved every one of these things in his mind. In his heart he knew the achievements were keeping him from following his energy, his heart, and doing what he needed to do in this world to be fulfilled. His 'goals' came from imposed views of how families 'should' be. From views around how much money one should acquire in a lifetime and how successful the whole deal is.

 So what is success? It's what I constantly rave about. Success is finding out who you are and following your heart. It may not be anything that looks like success to the world.

Some of the Princesses I talk about are struggling to find their way despite the fact that they look like they have everything. 'Being pretty doesn't make you happy' – what an old cliché! 'Having money doesn't make you happy' – another old cliché! If they are so old, why the hell does the world keep chasing after those two things and destroying everyone in their path?

A friend told me today she was watching a TV show where an author of a relationship book was being interviewed. He was chatting with the audience about relationships and a very pretty woman spoke about having an average relationship and she obviously wasn't happy. The author of this book said to her, "Honey, with your looks you can have anyone you want". Or something like that.

That is the absolute epitome of what is wrong with our world today. If we are that shallow, then we are in huge trouble! Why are we competing to the point of losing sight of everything else? When do we teach our kids compassion for themselves and others and about giving of themselves to create better lives for everyone?

All the competition does is create doubt in the mind of a person who has been brought up to believe their looks will make them a winner, or their money will make them a winner, or their work position will make them a winner. What happens when they are challenged? What happens when somebody doesn't agree that they are the prettiest thing ever? Or challenges their wealth, or their position? Would it trigger 'righteous indignation' that someone would dare to question how precious they are?

Underneath they have nothing to sustain them. It's confidence built on a lie. Their world crashes and they get resentful that life isn't treating them as it should. They start to build another, stronger case. They look for more people to support their false identity and so on it goes.

It's the same way the Gurus of the world look for people to build their lies and keep them safe as the ones that 'do' (know, that is).

I talked earlier in the book about the Wolves, the people who come to tell you all about your faults and precede the conversation by telling you how sensitive they are, how connected they are and that they can't deal with confrontation. They can't deal with confrontation, but they're happy to confront you with all that is wrong with you in the name of 'helping'. They've already set it up so that you can't confront them back because they are so 'sensitive'. These people are bullies. They are saying they are sensitive, but their energy is in complete control and knocking you all over the place to keep you in line.

We are building nations full of frauds. The fraud in us lies so deep it's almost impossible to understand.

I find that one of the first things people do when being confronted with a truth about themselves that they don't want to hear, is to gather troops to support their lies. I've had so many people come back to me and say things like, "You know how you said I was controlling? Well I've talked to lots of my friends and my mother (or boss or twenty other people) and they all say: "Oh no Fred, you're not controlling, you're a really nice person"."

If you've ever done that yourself – gone to look for support for your story – then I dare you to have a look at the thing you're gathering support for. Go on. What if feeling it and understanding it changes your life?

The other side of the coin is a man like my father who was so desperate to keep control of our family he used violence to do that. Fear-based lives are so common in today's world.

Some years ago, cousins of mine from Sydney came to visit. I hadn't seen them for a long time. We had lots of fun together when we were young and like everybody else they knew nothing about how we lived. They sat and told stories about my father, their uncle, that were a little difficult for me to hear. They talked about how gorgeous he was and how much they loved him and how helpful he had been to their families over the years. I guess for me there was a little sadness that I didn't know my father like that. He was able to share something with them that he couldn't share with us because of his need to control us. He didn't have that same agenda running with them. They were not 'his' family. If I feel this situation, and look around me in the world, it's such a theme. When two people enter into a relationship – any kind of relationship – there is that energetic contract they make with each other which allows this kind of behaviour to go on. Not only violence, but also manipulation, control, or the opposite – victim consciousness and apathy. It ruins lives instead of enhancing them.

When I first met Jeff and Tanya they were the 'perfect' married couple. They joined one of our programs and stated they weren't really sure why they'd joined, just that they thought it would be 'interesting'. I don't know about them, but it was interesting for me to watch a couple hold hands and kiss, spend every spare minute together attached at the hip and have absolutely no real connection. They spoke of their perfect life and their beautiful property and their very successful jobs with a kind of pride that came straight from their egos and the fact that they figured they had it all sorted. I looked at these guys and thought, "*Where the hell do I start with this big packet of illusion?*"

I jumped right in knowing it could be their last session with me if they weren't really committed to getting real. The fact was, they had put themselves in a room with me to be worked, so I guessed they were there for a reason. If I could think of a bigger word than 'shocked' right here I'd use it. They were shocked to their core at what I said to them. That they were isolated from each other as well as everyone else. That the 'holding hands' thing was an absolute fantasy as was the statement that they were 'okay' even though deep down they could not connect at all.

So here they were facing the dismantling of their picket fence. Tanya went into Victim and Jeff hit the Guru, the "I know everything, so how can you be right?" thing.

Their journey has been an ongoing process over the past year or so and you would have to hear from them what it was like to face this stuff. All I know is they had the courage to say, "What if this is true? What if we could have it all? The lifestyle? The property? A true ability to connect not only with each other but with the greater community? AND the Love?"

They have worked their butts off and gone to places that scared the living daylights out of them. Places where it looked at times like the relationship had absolutely no merit. They moved into separate rooms for a while and felt the truth of their own existence without the attachment of co-dependence. They worked through their co-dependence and their pulling each other's energy around to the point where they got really angry with each other. They kept going. All this was the truth, the truth of the illusion they had created behind their own special picket fence.

Today, I am happy to say these guys are one of the most real couples I've met in a long time. They are happy when they are happy and not happy when they are not happy. They are truthful and honest, hit walls, get back up and keep loving each other, really loving each other. They are committed to working on their relationship and neither of them put up with crap from each other or from themselves. They are both now volunteering in many community activities in their area and have felt the joy of giving to someone outside of themselves. It makes life so much simpler.

They keep working hard everyday and last month announced to us they are going to be parents. When I met Tanya she said kids were 'not her thing'. She didn't like them at all. Now she is an excited expectant mum. Her fear of kids was wrapped up in the big illusion of her life.

31

Judgement

DOING THE CO-DEPENDENT SHUFFLE WITH ARCHIE I GAINED A fair bit of weight. I don't know what happened really, it was like one day I was my normal self and the next day I was fat.

The funny thing about that is, on the inside I felt exactly the same. I guess every kilogram that I gained affected the way I looked physically but the inside did not change. I kept working, growing, counselling people, moving ahead and doing all the things that make me fulfilled in my life.

On the outside I was gaining weight. I wasn't all that happy about it, but something didn't quite register into the energy part of me. My mind said it was fine, I'd never really been overweight and it wouldn't be a problem.

I still don't truthfully know today if it has been a problem, because I have learned enormous amounts about people and the way they judge each other for how they look. If I hadn't been overweight I would have still been one of those people who said I didn't judge people, but in the get-down-and-dirty truth I looked at a photo of myself one day and thought, *"Christ I look like one of those fat people I feel sorry for."* That was outrageous. I knew better than that.

It's funny, the weight thing. You feel like exactly the same person you've always been, then you feel someone's energy dismissing you or having that sympathy thing going on because you're fat. It's a weird feeling fighting your mind that says, *"Why are they looking at me like that?"* Or dealing with the odd glance sideways from friends or clients that says you really ought to be looking after yourself better.

A friend I'd known for a long time once said to me she didn't want to walk in front of me looking like she did in case I was embarrassed. I explained to her that I didn't feel anything at all about her body. That was her issue.

The reasons why I put on weight are quite apparent to me now. The feeling inside, as I start to get back to my normal weight, is almost like *'where did I go for those years? How did I manage to keep working and learning and fighting for my Soul while my body did something else?'*

I mentioned that it has been very helpful to have been overweight and it has. The strength I have gained from being able to stand up in who I am regardless of the bulges that I carried has been incredible. That wasn't always the case and I went through times where I felt the pressure of my clothes being too tight. Or buying a bigger size and wondering what people thought. Then I went through the 'who cares anyway?'' phase. Having Arch around was easy because he didn't care about the body factor.

I went along to a Personal Trainer to begin the journey back to my physical self and it was great to work with Mandi on the points where I got stuck and felt the sabotage come and to then discuss that with her. For Mandi, it was a learning in working with someone who actually knew that they were about to sabotage, and was open about the 'old stuff' coming in and pulling them off track. I even went to the trouble of injuring myself quite badly, limping around for three months or so, until I understood where the injury began and what I was hiding from way back then. Same old vulnerability issue, by the way.

All of that has helped me to gain strength for me and to build that place inside stronger and stronger. That place that knows who I am and what I am here to do. The place that allows me to be open to following my energy without the fear of being out of control.

Last week I went to the Gold Coast to visit Tim and Cassie and help them move into their new home. I also ran a training on the Sunshine Coast while I was there. I spent some time wandering around the place observing things.

One afternoon I climbed out of the pool and was heading out of the door to go to the shops. The weather was steamy. I pulled on a singlet and short pants and as I passed the mirror it crossed my mind that I'd be pleased to get back to my normal weight. I didn't go any further with that but it did cross my mind. Then I forgot about it and went to Woolies to get things organised for dinner.

As I got out of the car and headed towards the supermarket I watched a couple walk out of there. The woman was probably my age, early fifties. She was gorgeous. She was one of those women you have a second look at. She had the whole Queensland look really – blonde, brown skin, gorgeous body.

As they passed me I saw the lines of worry on her face and felt the anger coming from her partner or at least, the man she was with. I couldn't help but hear her pleading to be heard. He spoke in a very loud voice as he accused her of being angry amongst other things. She caved in completely. By the time she got to the car, with many heads now turning their way, she was almost in a foetal position apologizing profusely for her wrong-doings.

What the hell is that about? So where do the body and the looks get people when they are under pressure?

Mandi once shared with me that a lot of her friends in the body building business, all of whom have incredible bodies, eat healthy food consistently and exercise every day, die suddenly when they get to around fifty or sixty. That didn't surprise me at all. People who have only their bodies and their egos cannot survive if they get a wrinkle, or if their boobs drop, or they gain a kilogram.

We laughed a lot about Mandi shouting at all her clients in her classes to get their posture right. She'd yell "TTG!" I asked what that meant and Mandi explained, "Tits to God". My daughter Niki, who also trains hard at the gym, has a great body and knows Mandi well said, "Once you've had kids the TTG is actually 'Tits to Ground' from then on in".

The 'looking good' thing is so rampant in our society. I believe it's responsible for so much of our teenage suicide rate, depression and anxiety alongside a host of other things.

What if, when we got dressed up to go out, we only dressed for ourselves? What if, when we looked at someone, we looked for their essence inside of them, instead of at the package?

 What if the thing that shines from inside us, that unique place that is our flame, our Spirit, our passion for living, is enough for us? Then, no matter what judgment was dished out by another, it would not snuff out our flame.

What if that essence was what we allowed people to see, rather than the fat or thin bodies, the make-up that covers us, the cardboard cut-out for every occasion?

Then it wouldn't matter at all if someone commented on our appearance. Right now, whether the comment is negative or positive it affects people. They are either looking for praise or fearful of the negative comment that will drag them down.

In their fight for survival, the 'looking good', 'special' type people will go straight to their egos if challenged and judge the person challenging them. It's one big competition really. The trouble is it has no end.

I heard a story today in a training I'm running from a nurse who works in palliative care. At present, she is working with a client who is in the last stages of his life, and his wife has given the staff a list of instructions as to how to get him ready for visitors. What he has to wear, how he is to look! This guy is about to die, all he wants is peace and some space to feel what is happening to him. Prepare, if you like, to go across. According to his wife, his hospital gown is not appropriate attire for receiving visitors. He needs to be dressed up and looking 'spiffy'. I'm not sure how you do that in the last days of your life? In my experience, you get a whole other 'glow' at that stage of your life, if you are given the chance to die surrounded by truth and Love.

The staff are furious and are telling her it's very difficult to keep changing him into clothes when he's in pain. It falls on deaf ears. She is relentless. His neighbours arrived to see him recently but he'd made it very clear to the staff that he did not want to see anyone. These people were incensed and an hour later the wife was on the phone furious that they had driven all the way to see him and they weren't allowed in.

I'm speechless. No I'm not really. This is just one

of the many crippling things going on in our society every single day, right under our noses and nobody even takes any notice. Or, if they do, they wouldn't dare say anything in case they themselves didn't look good, or they rocked the boat too hard. The question I would ask is what went on during their relationship that allowed those things to happen in the end? Where was their love, the respect and the true communication?

Judgment is another crippler in our society. I hear so many people say "I don't judge others". What a crock! Within five minutes you will hear twenty slight judgments come out of their mouth. Even if that judgment comes wrapped in sugar. It may only be a look. At the end of the day judgment is really about positioning yourself somewhere. "Am I better? Am I worse? Could I take that person on? Can I gain power over that person? If not, I'll find a fault so I can feel more powerful".

A few years ago a client came to me who had done a lot of work with the esoteric communities. She had lots of pieces of paper to prove she knew a lot. She was in a group I was running on an ongoing basis and was quite blown out at what she was learning about herself. In her own words, she had to find something out about me so she could invalidate the learning, something that would allow her to slip back into the comfortable esoteric stuff that didn't really challenge the essence of who she was.

It's not hard to find that kind of information with me. I don't put on airs and graces. The afternoon tea was served with lots of lovely food, but for this woman it was the answer to her prayers. I served Kraft dip from the supermarket with some crackers. That's all she needed. I felt her arrogance rise up but I didn't challenge her at that point. It wasn't until a month or so later that she sheepishly brought up in the group that she judged the hell out of me for serving Kraft dip. Apparently it wasn't conducive to someone who was 'spiritual'. Good Lord! The things people think up in their heads. Just for the record I love Kraft dip and continue to serve it whenever I feel like it.

Judgment is a constant. It's another thing that we *constantly* deny.

Let's rock the boat. Let's get it all out in the open and see what comes of that.

32

The Co=dependent Shuffle

DURING THE WRITING THIS BOOK I'VE BEEN PUT IN FRONT of loads of couples who are doing the co-dependent shuffle very nicely, and denying it, of course. It got me thinking about how that all worked with Arch and I. Why I felt the need somewhere inside to gain weight for a time and see how that worked?

The other reason I'm inspired to share this very personal part of my life is for the kids of the world.

My kids weren't affected that much by my relationship with Arch, because I made it clear up front that I would deal with them and their issues. He could make whatever relationship he needed to with them in his own right, which I would not be involved in. They were teenagers at that stage and knew enough about themselves to know what was right or wrong for them. They had a good relationship with their father so didn't need to substitute Arch for anything they were lacking in.

It was made very clear to Arch that if there were any hints of standing over them, or trying to manipulate them in any way, his bags would be on the front door step before he could blink. I wouldn't have a clue if that was the 'right' or 'wrong' attitude. It was what it was. What it did for my kids was allow them to build strong independent relationships with him based on their own feelings rather than on anything to do with me.

They still have good relationships with him now. He often goes to the Gold Coast from his home in Gympie to work with Tim when he's busy. But actually even if they didn't have good relationships with him it is no concern of mine.

I have many clients with children who go through massive transition with a new partner, husband or wife that I believe is unnecessary. The adults get way too involved in trying to please the new person in their life and a lot of the time the kids get lost somewhere. Or the kids have to deal with an overbearing person coming into their lives who often has no idea about how to raise kids themselves, but makes sure they have a lot of opinions about it. There's a whole workshop in this.

Arch and I had been friends twenty years ago. He was a friend of a friend and we got on well. When I met him this time he was down in Melbourne, visiting those same friends and we caught up for dinner. I was working as a counsellor at the time, travelling around the country a lot with my work. I had just finished a lot of training.

The details don't matter. What actually happened was that Arch paid me a lot of attention which freaked me out a little, but there was something about him that I felt safe with. Not too far down the track he moved back to Melbourne and we tentatively started seeing each other. We had a lot in common in some areas. He loved Nature. He was a great gardener, a great cook and he wanted to take care of me. Weird concept really. I was very capable of taking care of myself.

I remember the first time he walked out of the house and got into the drivers seat of my new car. My first thought was, *"How dare you!"* but the other part of me was trying to say *'maybe I have to put up with this in relationships?* I battled a lot that day, sitting in the passenger seat being really angry and wanting to say, "This is my bloody car, don't assume things".

I hadn't been in a relationship for a long time, so I guessed I had a lot to learn and had to stop being so beastly independent. In hindsight I needed to step up right there and then and say the things I was feeling.

I found myself in the precarious position of not always speaking up, which was incredibly new for me. I did discuss all these things with him after the event but there always seemed to be a plausible answer so I relented at times. Not always, but at times. It's often difficult in relationships to know if you are standing up for your rights or whether you are being a bully. When you are sharing and when you are just plain taking. The line is faded so the learning is intense.

The other side to our relationship was that we were extremely different people. His life in Queensland had been a very relaxed, very social one. My life consisted of work and more work. Even though I'd had the head injury I tailored my work to working from home and doing group work with different types of people. I didn't have a lot of memory but it wasn't an issue, as tracking energy and getting under stories is simply a feeling thing, not a thinking thing. My focus has always been my job. I take it seriously. My Soul journey is of primary importance to me and my work is a huge part of that.

Arch supported my work wholeheartedly and was happy to 'keep the home fires burning' while I travelled and did my job. So we puddled along for the first few years and were happy to be together doing whatever we did. We probably weren't your average couple. We didn't do a lot of socialising, but we spent a lot of time in Nature and loads of time planting gardens, including amazing fruit and vegetables. We dug ponds the size of dams and enjoyed all the rewards that kind of simple life brings.

As far as our sex life went it was pretty well non-existent and that suited me fine. We were buddies and it worked well. Arch had suffered a massive stroke a few years before and it had affected his ability to have a physical relationship with anyone. That's the story any-way. The truth will be revealed further in the chapter.

Having said that, we did experience some great moments together, but neither of us were into pretend-ing it was someone else, and I didn't go for biting the sheet and hoping like hell it was over. I'm never going to do that. If I want to have sex I will, if I don't I sim-ply won't. Arch was the same and as much as it caused some 'stuff' in the beginning, when you're tentatively getting the relationship going and it sucks to be told you're not wanted, it taught me to see the whole picture and not just the precious 'what about me? don't you love me?' thing.

During the last two years of our relationship the energy for the actual relationship was done. We still lived together and did things for each other. We still laughed and talked and went walking together, but the energy was done.

We hadn't been in the same bedroom for quite a long time, but we did enjoy a lot of that time being friends and learning how to part without fuss. There was something in the 'being friends' though. It was still being friends and supporting the negative part of our relationship. The part where deep-down there was something that didn't want to grow outside of the relationship. We were in that comfort zone where stepping right up into walking forward on your journey is foiled by the patterns of safety.

These patterns are so deeply ingrained they are very difficult to see. It's easy for me to see them in others, it was a little tricky to see them in myself because I was one of the people who didn't want to step up completely. I obviously had something invested in staying where I was. Even though I am out there in the world and I do lots of branch-shaking, there were still those much deeper parts I was avoiding.

So we continued to play that game. I would speak up to Arch a lot, as is my way. He would not respond, as is his way. I got sick of raving on so I shut up in the end. I did my best to hear that he processed things differently to me and that he needed time to come up with an answer to my questions, or a response to me telling him that I was pretty 'over' certain things. I tried desperately to feel it from his perspective but two months for one answer and I'm done. Over a period of years that builds into resentment.

During the last year it became apparent that the co-dependence we had created in certain areas was kicking in hard. As it panned-out, Arch was the one who was leaving the home and he went into a lot of fear around living without the relationship. Actually, living without the co-dependence was probably a more accurate description, even though he agreed we had shut down huge parts of ourselves to exist in this relationship in the last few years.

He often got angry and I did my best to hold the compassion I honestly felt for him in this situation. We still talked through it, but I have to say it became tedious, and a few months before he left we did go into battle. He got very upset one night and I had just about had enough of the 'dragging things out', so there was a bit of yelling and blaming.

The next day we sorted through it and saw how easy it could be to make this bitter. I was craving my independence and he was hanging on for grim death but it allowed him to then talk about his fears and we were able to be clear about where we both stood and understand the fears of the other.

The week he left was a very sad week for us both. He decided to go interstate as it made it easier for him to cope with the break-up. I drove him to the airport to catch the plane and we had to stop before we got there as we both sobbed at what we were about to do.

Still, inside, I knew this was the only way. It was right. There was no turning back. I knew the sobbing lay in the co-dependence because in my heart it was clearly the right decision.

I guess, looking back, everything that happened for us as individuals helped us to learn and grow. And the fact was we were actually eighty per cent happy. I looked around and couldn't see many other couples who were any more than eighty per cent happy. Most weren't even that happy, so I figured we had some good stuff going on. And we did. We talked a lot and I worked on our issues. It would have been helpful if he'd done that too... It was a great feeling for me to come home from a two-day full-on workshop and know there would be a gorgeous meal on the table, the house would be clean, Daniel would be organised and I could relax with Arch by the pond and not worry about anything else.

He said he was very happy doing this for a long time, however, when there was an issue to confront, and I'm not shy about confronting issues, he would pull out the fact that he was bored and wanted to do something besides take care of me.

And the shuffle begins again.

In the beginning I didn't want him to take care of me. I was often angry that he would do everything before I had the chance to. Then I got used to it, and in the end I was angry if I had to do those things myself.

My part in taking care of him was in working and providing the money in the household. That wasn't everyone's idea of how it worked but it worked for us for a long time. When I ran workshops from home Arch would cook for twenty or more people and do it very well. He built beautiful furniture and worked for Tim at times to give him some extra money. All in all we were having a good time together. From the outside looking in we were a very happy couple. Even from the inside, we did not have the bitterness or the fighting or even the distance between us that I see in a lot of relationships.

I hear couples tell me they love each other and

are happy most of the time – look at Jeff and Tanya when they first started working on themselves. It's garbage and they mostly know it inside, they just hide it behind the smiles and the perhaps twenty per cent of happiness they can grab. The other eighty per cent is usually full of those little moments like the one when Arch drove my car, those moments that get locked deep down into resentment. Or into the 'it's not worth bringing it up' place, which sits beside the 'they wouldn't understand' and the 'it's all too hard' places.

As I've said before, marriage busters.

Then of course there are the people who stay like that forever and die unhappy because they didn't do anything about it.

It's the twenty per cent that Arch and I didn't have that eventually ended our relationship. That twenty per cent where I wasn't being challenged. Which, by the way, is actually the reason I chose Arch in the beginning. I was prepared to work to a certain level in those years but not beyond that. At the beginning of this chapter I mentioned that I had a very safe feeling around Arch. I didn't know what the safe feeling was then. Now I do. I wasn't being challenged in that twenty per cent in a way that would help me to stand up and grow.

We challenged each other in lots of areas, more than most I suspect but it wasn't the kind of challenge I needed. We were comfortable – very, very comfortable, but still just comfortable.

I believe Arch chose me for that same reason. I'll confront any issue and I'm challenging in a lot of ways, but the areas Arch was hiding from, like the physical stuff and the reasons behind his lack of interest, was left untouched for a while because it suited me to do that. I didn't want to go there either and so it didn't seem important at all. Therein lie the subtleties of co-dependence.

Eventually, we looked at it a bit closer and talked it through, and Arch realised that there was a lot of control in the fact that he'd had a stroke and could not have sex. He looked at his life and understood that he had felt manipulated in relationships around sex. He felt as though if he was a good boy and did all the right things he would be rewarded with sex. If he wasn't he was punished. That's his story, but it made sense.

There's yet another book to be written about how men and women and also their soul genders relate in these areas. How Arch withdrew his energy and withheld the physical stuff to keep control of that very personal part of his life.

Within the twenty per cent is the place where the

work gets done. That's where the contentment lies. I'm talking about the deep contentment where the passion for life and relationship lives. As opposed to apathy or denial. Or comfort-zone relationships. Where the absolute truth is hidden, albeit slightly, but still hidden so the true work in relationships is avoided.

Arch and I worked very well to a certain level, then the co-dependence would kick in to keep us safe. It's the 'numbness versus passion, choose your team' quote that we use in Muragai (my life strategies business).

The choice lies in accepting the Picket Fence and all that it entails, or being truthful enough to say 'I need to keep challenging myself'. It's in confronting the small and large things that sabotage true connection. It's in owning your personal responsibility and never blaming another for things that go wrong. It's in knowing that you, yourself, will create them to keep the drama going to stay away from that deeper truth.

Within the deeper truth we have to stand up fully. We have to own every single energetic interaction and our part in it. We have to know we one hundred per cent create our own reality. Good or bad. We are creating it. I know a lot of people who say they understand that but in their energy they are still looking for someone to blame at some level.

It had been a really busy week. Arch had been

gone for some months now and I was doing the 'work, Daniel, dog, fish, housework' thing. It was very tedious at times and I had experienced some really hectic cases in my practice. It was Friday night and I had a training starting the next morning. Hayesy was out for the night and it was likely I would get a call at 2 am to pick him up. The dog had been sick; one of the fish had died through the week. All in all I was in overwhelm.

Arch rang that night and for a moment I opened a door, slightly, but still opened that door that said energetically, "Boy, this is hard without you". He picked up on it and talked about understanding how I felt and being there for me. I felt the uncomfortable feeling in my energy, I knew I was fudging. However I kept going. It felt good to have someone understand what it's like to be under this particular pressure.

When I woke up the next morning I felt terrible. I knew I had pulled him in to have a whinge and I also knew he would listen and support me. But where did that leave him?

It was a really selfish thing to do to him. The next day he rang again and asked how I was and again got into supporting me. I had to tell him up front I had been self-serving and precious the night before and had pulled him in to support my crap.

I was very capable of doing things myself – but

one bad day and I was pulling at him. It was inexcusable and I apologized for my thoughtlessness. Arch had hooked onto that feeling of being able to support me and I guess people could say 'what's wrong with that?' But I knew that wasn't where I wanted to head and that I had used him to serve my wants. It wasn't clean and I knew it. All it would create would be to set up the same thing we had in the relationship – supporting each other's wants instead of our needs. It also didn't give me the opportunity to sit in the overwhelm and feel what it was I truly needed to do to find the way out for myself.

Of course there is a real place for people to support each other cleanly. That's not what that story is about. However, supporting cleanly entails each person supporting the other with no attachment whatsoever to the outcome or to how that other person lives their life. Even in relationships. We don't have ownership over others. As I've said before if you have an opinion about how another is living their life you don't respect that person. Where there is no respect there is no Love.

33

John

I'VE NEVER BEEN SURE HOW TO WRITE THIS CHAPTER ABOUT my relationship with 'John'. John is my teacher and my friend. My Spirit Mentor, I guess, is the best term to use.

If this all sounds a bit 'airy-fairy' read on. It's an absolutely raw and honest account of how this has played out in my life and the amazing consequences of being blessed enough to have this kind of guidance.

I have just finished a three-day training with seventeen people from all over the country. As we finished the last session of the day I stood back as these people danced and cried and hugged, and I knew in my heart their lives were a thousand times better for being in that room for three days with our team. I also knew I could never have held up that kind of transformation without John walking with me.

I understood all of a sudden what he had been telling me for the past three years and patiently waiting for me to get. It has inspired me to talk about John, which, up until now, I do very little of. Talk about him that is.

I'm going to tell this exactly how it happened. In starting out I'd like to explain something. I knew people had Spirit teachers. I had read lots of books about the subject and never doubted that what I read was true for those people.

My honest opinion back then was that it was for someone else, definitely not for me. I was not then, and am not now, an 'airy-fairy' person. I'm pretty grounded, down-to-earth and a realist. Even though in my darkest times I believed in God and I believed angels were helping me and my family. I taught my children about angels and how to feel the support and love that exists for us within Nature and from angels and also from God. That all felt very real and very safe.

JOHN

The night John first spoke to me was the biggest shock I'd had for many years. I was woken up; I sat bolt upright in bed and his voice was loud and very real. He said to me, "I want you to work with me." I convinced myself it was a dream and tried to find sleep again. That wasn't going to happen. My heart raced. I turned the light on as I figured if he was going to materialise I'd feel a lot safer if I wasn't in the dark.

Over the next weeks I experienced sensations during the night of floating out of my body and looking around my house from the roof. This totally freaked me out. I'd wake up with such a jolt in the bed that I'd shake and, at times, vomit for hours. I started having anxiety attacks and not wanting to go to bed. I must have shut it out fairly well because all I could ever remember for some weeks or even months was the anxiety and consequently the sickness in the middle of the night. I didn't dare talk to anyone about this as I figured they'd think I had totally lost the plot.

At the time I was seeing clients from home, and as I was working with people I would hear John's voice telling me different things about these people and how to work with them. It made life easier, but I was fighting very hard at this point to deny everything that was happening. I tried very hard to convince my-self it was really just my own voice talking in my head.

I believed I had very strong Knowing, but I had to convince myself this wasn't real to stay sane for a bit.

It's hard for me to explain how this sounded. Suffice to say, when John spoke, I eventually sat up and took notice. As he started teaching me about things and telling me what they had planned for me, I must have sounded extremely boring and repetitive for him as I remember saying over and over again, "Why me? I'm just here living in Montrose. I don't know much". My thought was I knew a lot of esoteric people who talked about their guides and I'd had massages where people had said my guides were there saying things. I didn't really believe them then and now as I write this I'm still not sure if I do. My not listening was never about not respecting him. Well, I guess it was, but it was definitely more about me not believing in me.

John's guidance is unmistakable. He speaks about relevant every day things right through to planetary things but always with a clarity I can understand. When I kept asking, "Why me?" he kept saying, "You can relate to all kinds of people, people from every walk of life. The rich and the poor alike. You are ordinary and people will listen to you when you teach this in the world." I just had to trust that he knew what he was talking about, as what he was saying was a long, long way from my reality.

Not long after he started talking to me he told me I needed to write a book about my life. Put everything in it and also what I'd learned. It's taken me four years to put pen to paper and lots of excuses and denying the fact that I was actually being instructed to do this. I did say he was patient.

Today I know why I resisted the writing of the book. It's certainly bringing up lots of emotions. Lots of energy around what I've created to get my lessons.

I'm going to write about a couple of things that happened in those early days that had me reeling for months. Remember I'm your ordinary person on the street. I'd dabbled in meditation here and there but this was a whole new concept for me to absorb.

I dreamed one night that I was walking along the road where we lived. It was dark and I came across two beautiful horses that were running along the road, obviously broken free from their paddock. It felt dangerous, as cars wouldn't see them. I went to them and led them back to their paddock and put a wire up so they couldn't escape again. I woke the next morning with a clear memory of that dream... and the smell of horses in my bedroom. "Very weird", I thought.

An hour or so later, as it was just beginning to get light, I was sitting on our front verandah when I spotted Arch and another guy across the road fixing a fence. When he came back home I asked what he'd been doing. He told me the two horses in the paddock had broken out last night. Someone had put them back but the fence needed proper repairing. He was assisting the guy to do that.

I sat frozen to that chair for three hours. I didn't dare move. Not sure why, just that absolute terror took over my mind. *"How could that be? It couldn't. It wasn't possible. Did I just dream what happened and someone else put them in the paddock?"* I'm still not sure to this day, but later that day, after finally getting out of the chair, I went with lots of gusto into the garden and asked John very firmly: "What happened last night? Why did you make me go and do that? Did I do that? Why there? Why in my street?" A million questions at once. He said simply, "If we'd taken you to save a child in India would you have believed it?" "No", was all I could muster.

I thought about this for a while. Asked lots of questions now. Started understanding that if I really had something to do for Spirit I'd better start listening and believing, or I'd be completely disrespecting the fact that they were talking to me at all.

By the way, the reason I call him 'John' is that in the beginning when he was speaking to me constantly I said to him "You're talking to me every day; I need to call you something". He said "What do you need to call me?" and I said "I don't know, how about 'John'?" and he said "As you will."

Later on, when it became clear that 'John' is not who he is, he said "You were afraid back then and you needed to feel comfortable. This had to be simple for you. That's why you needed to call me John."

There are literally hundreds of stories now that could fill this chapter. Really, all I want to get across is that this stuff really does happen even though I fought against it for a long time. Why? Fear I guess. Fear of being out of control. I had a funny moment standing on the balcony one morning listening to John talk about starting my company, why and how, and what I was meant to be teaching about. I listened intently then something terrifying dropped into my head. I said to him, "I'm okay with this so far John, not too freaked out, but one thing I have to say is don't be talking through me with your voice. You know how those people pass out and another voice comes through them? That would spin me out completely". There was a long silence and he replied, "That won't happen." I often wonder in the silence whether he is either laughing so hard he can't respond or rolling his eyes in disbelief at my resistance.

John has since introduced me to other mentors who have assisted me with very specific issues.

From having John in my life I have been challenged to the absolute edge about my beliefs, how they had limited me in lots of areas. My fear and how we live within our fears to keep us safe. Sounds crazy doesn't it. Live with 'fear' to keep us safe. Safe from what??

My work has been enhanced enormously through my guidance. Things I would never have dreamed of have come through to work with and I watch as people connect to this level of guidance and soar.

I even got to write a song. John said to me on a number of occasions, "You need to write a song that will take people into a deeper feeling place". We use a lot of music in our work so it made sense, but I never dreamed I would be writing it. I laughed a bit about this. I wondered whether Spirit mentors understood that there are things we can do and things that we can't do.

One morning I woke with some things I would like to say in a song and it went from there. I wrote pages of lyrics and just at the same time was introduced to a wonderful songwriter and musician from Brisbane. Bill, and my friend of twenty years, Trish, took the words and turned them into a beautiful song.

The phoenix rising from the ashes was the theme I had chosen. It asks people if they have the courage to find their truth and speak it and was what I wanted conveyed. The song is now called The Phoenix Rises.

It was a month or so of sending lyrics backwards and forwards to Brisbane. Bill and Trish came down with all Bill's equipment and we set up a studio in my lounge room and started recording. A few days later Bill went home with all he needed to produce the most amazing CD, which is now used in workshops and with clients. It's a constant reminder to people that there is more if you are willing to reach for it. Trish and my daughter Niki sing and my grandchildren, Toby and Chelsea, have a speaking part in the middle of the song. This was also directed by John.

I was driving Toby home from kindergarten one day and he looked tired. I rubbed his hair and said to him, "Is my grandson tired?" He responded, "I'm not your grandson." I said, "Is my little blue eyes tired?" "I'm not your little blue eyes". This banter went on for a minute or two when he turned and looked at me and said very clearly, "My name is Toby, let me be who I came here to be."

It floored me for a second then John said straight away, "That needs to go into the song." Lots of words from John were clearly spoken and written into the lyrics. It was heaps of fun and proved to me yet again

I only need to trust and stop listening to my head and I can achieve whatever I'm asked to.

It was Christmas 2004 when I asked John for the next step. I'd been working with him and others for some years now and felt like there was more I needed to know. That's what I love the most about John. He asks me to do things then waits while I go through the process and actually achieve what he's asked. People say you will never be asked to do anything you are not ready for. Well I'm not so sure.

Christmas Eve was a lonely night for me. Lonely, that's a funny word. I love being on my own. In fact I crave being on my own. Hardly ever get to be alone and when that time comes I cherish it. I sat outside with a glass of 'red'. Daniel was in Bairnsdale for Christmas. I had worked long and hard on the company's new website and it was all finished. I'd had copious amounts of clients leading up to Christmas so not much time to sit and think. Things in the business were exciting.

Still there was that empty feeling. I hadn't had that feeling for years. "Okay John, I'm ready for the next step. Bring it on. I'm fearless about my Soul journey. No matter what it takes I'm going to do it."

I wasn't prepared for what came.

34

Ian — take 47

THAT'S EXACTLY WHAT WRITING THIS CHAPTER IS LIKE FOR ME.

Up front? I asked for the next step and did not like what I got one bit. This last year has been the culmination of all the learning I've ever done in this life. It's the culmination of all the times I got close to deep connection and knocked myself out.

It's also the beginning of taking on board all the lessons I learned from the Teacher that I had somehow up until now only understood in my head. And of course understanding it in your head is a total waste of time until you can really understand it in your energy. Then you may begin to understand it on a Soul level.

I've almost taken this chapter out of the book so many times for all kinds of reasons. Right up to today when we are twenty four hours from hitting the 'Send' button to the publisher, with not only the manuscript that has taken four years to come to fruition, but with all the technical information a publisher needs to produce the fine detail of a book. Information that has been painstakingly put together by the amazing team of people I work closely with.

One of those reasons is that it is almost impossible to explain the depth of the feelings I have experienced and the copious amounts of tears I have cried from the gratitude at having had this lesson presented to me in this way.

Another reason is that the lessons have been learned from a man I knew a very long time ago from Queensland who knows nothing about this apart from a brief conversation I had with him six months ago.

However, I will push on. Again, to make things clear. The man I speak of in this chapter has no knowledge of these lessons I experience on a daily basis. It is not about him. I could have used any name here, and I tried that, but for me energetically it wasn't the same.

I knew him years ago and he challenged me on a

human level to the point where I could not stand the sight of him. I know now that was only my 'stuff' and my reaction to him. He represented a lot of things in men I couldn't tolerate. I did not and would not give him the time of day. I guess he was the most arrogant man I'd encountered in a long time. And I'm guessing he wouldn't even have registered that I didn't give him the time of day.

Ironic then, that when I ask God and John for the next level of learning for my Soul journey, it is this man that appears in my dreams six nights a week. Obviously in their wisdom they needed to send an energy of someone I had known, put a face to it and even a voice so that the learning would be real for me.

I can't explain how it has been and how it still is today. It is intense, personal and very raw. I will do my best to convey this part of my learning but hang in if it gets a little weird and spare a thought for how weird it is for me to have this energy around me constantly teaching me things about myself that I know are the absolute truth.

It might be productive to point out here again that I am the grounded realist. I don't believe anything unless I experience it myself. It took me three years to get comfortable with John being with me and teaching me. Now this!!

If there was any way I could have avoided, de-nied, or got out of these lessons in the first six months I would have run for the hills – and I often tried. The thing with this kind of learning is that his energy would just follow me. My next tactic would have been to be really strong and aggressive in my energy which would push most people away in an instant. Even though I don't use that aggressive energy any more, it was something I tried at the beginning of this many many times. This guy, Ian, would stand and look at me with a calm look on his face and absolutely no intention of being intimidated by me.

This wasn't going well.

The dreams were precise and specific. They started with me walking on a beach. Ian walked up and held my hand. My head went insane. The thoughts I had in that moment were outrageous. But when my mind stopped for a brief second, I felt more safe and peace-ful somehow than I'd ever felt before.

I did not like this dream at all and got up at 3.00 am to tell John this must be a mistake. I was never going to learn anything from this man, he was not get-ting anywhere near me, even if it was just in a dream. I said "I'm assuming I'm meant to be learning about allowing men in at that much deeper place? Well good luck with that because I'm not budging on this one".

Rather rude of me to talk to John like that I know, but I've got limits and this was way over that limit. Having said all of this, somewhere deep inside me I obviously called Ian in, knowing he would be the only one who could take me on to get me to that next level.

I knew clearly this was about healing whatever wounds were left in me to heal. Emotional wounds. So I could walk forward again. John in his wisdom sent Ian to me this way as any real-life man walking through my door to teach me this deep intimate stuff would not have had a hope in Hades of getting close to me. I'm too good at the game for that. I don't want to play it anymore but if push comes to shove I'm great at ducking and weaving.

Here I'd like to talk about what I mean about deep intimate stuff. I don't mean sex, relationships, half-arsed marriages, or partnerships with a thousand attachments. I have talked a lot about that place inside each one of us that is unique. That spark that can fuel our lives with passion and joy if we are tough enough to find it and work with it. That's what I'm talking about.

I have done a truck load of work towards that place and I know I have made serious inroads. My work has been enhanced triple fold; my ability to help others has now been brought into much sharper perspective. I am able to see the places I was fudging in my work.

I'm sure if this learning had been on a completely personal level I would never have entertained it. But I knew in my heart that if I could get through the kicking and screaming then this learning was definitely about my courage to not just look at this journey for myself, but always outside of myself. What part could I play in helping the world look at things from a different perspective?

Based on results, everything we've tried so far has failed miserably. Or worked to a certain degree then it gets too close to home and we lose the plot again.

I am fierce about my Soul journey and the level of Love and compassion I can share in the world. But until this experience with Ian (well with me and Ian's energy around me) I had not been challenged to look at those places we all convince ourselves are 'okay'.

I wish I had a whole book to explain what this has been like and it would take that to do the job. Each dream would last a month or so, five or six nights a week. All clear and precise. Then I would be given songs to listen to that would relate to those dreams. In the beginning, the lyrics were things I didn't want to hear but I would be asked to listen to them time and time again until I got the meaning. If I refused to listen, they'd be on the car radio or playing in a shop. And by the way, none of these songs are in the current Top Thirty Thousand, they are mainly songs from 'way back'.

All of this was about one very specific issue I had fudged on in my life. 'Fudged' meaning just letting it slip a little. Working hard and furiously on my journey but then allowing that little tiny bit at the end where we say, 'Oh well, I've done really well, I'll be okay'.

It was not okay for me anymore. I needed to step right up into the place where I am able and prepared for every door in front of me that leads to fulfilling my Soul's purpose here to open before me. And to walk through and take responsibility for what I've created and what I'm here to do. No more excuses.

Whether that be continuing my business with its' writing and teaching. Living my life in the Dandenong Ranges in Melbourne surrounded by my children, grandchildren and my gorgeous Daniel, or giving all of that up and washing elephants in India, or exploring the deeper issues of intimacy in relationship and teaching that. I need to have the courage to do this....

I need to show my grandchildren the way forward. I want them to have the courage to hold their Place in the Boat and know how to fight for it. I had to accept this learning as difficult as it was at first. Actually it was only difficult for my head and my ego.

After six months of these intense dreams with very specific learnings attached, and after I had actually stopped kicking and screaming full time. I started to feel a place in me that was stronger than I'd felt before.

Perhaps I could explain here that in the past few years since John has been guiding me my dreams are such that I can ask for guidance on a very specific issue and it will appear in my dreams as clear as a bell. Not like the dreams where you wake up wondering what it means and look up dream books or consult psychics, they are very rarely like that. Ninety-nine per cent of my dreams happen as though I'm walking in them and I know I am and the issue I have asked about is glaringly obvious.

What I started to understand at this stage was that John was asking me to know, understand and love someone underneath all the drama of the world. All the behaviour that we operate from. All the mind chatter that keeps us stuck or safe, whichever the case may be. He was asking me to trust him enough to go under my own mind and all the stories I had built and told myself about this man for eleven years, and go to a place inside of me where I could find love for him.

What a challenge! If I could soften my heart where he was concerned, I could do it for anyone else on the planet.

Here I was being given an opportunity on a very consistent basis to see how I operated under this kind of pressure. And let me tell you it was pressure, given the opinions and the feelings I'd had about this guy for so many years.

Not only do I dream about him very often, but I feel his energy at the most unexpected times, for example while I'm working or driving the car. I feel the energy around me and there is absolutely no mistaking it and my own energy will expand somehow – I feel lifted up or something. For a long time my head would kick in and start raving, but John would always say to me – and still does, "Settle. Feel, don't think. Don't look with your eyes. It's not in the seeing, it's in the Knowing".

So how this worked and still does today is that I will dream these particular dreams for a month or so until I stop fighting. Let me say here I now try and stop fighting within the month and sometimes that's fine, but when it comes to the very sensitive vulnerable areas I go back to kicking and screaming a little.

There were many things I listened to on that weekend with that incredible Teacher. I listened and understood in my head as I've said. What I believe now is that Ian was sent to take me through the energy of each one of those things spoken about in that training and much more than that.

I would constantly ask John why it had to be him. I frantically wrote a list of other men I knew that I would be able to learn from. Very short list I might add. John said simply, "Would any of those men challenge you like this?" I thought of not answering but of course the answer was "No".

 I was told that this way was necessary to be able to surrender my heart beyond the lies the world has created to keep people safe in co-dependent relationships that were not serving them.

Pretty big concept for me really.

Then I had a dream for a week or so where dead people (including Jo and a good friend Robyn who had just passed over) came to me and asked me to hold them. They were stone cold, of course and at first I was a little freaked-out by it. I was told I needed to touch people with Love now. That the world was cold and I needed to work from a truly loving and compassionate place.

This was okay but more and more Ian came to teach me about how to do this. My greatest argument at this stage was still that I knew this guy years ago and he was not loving as far as I was concerned. In fact he was arrogant and rude and ran that 'special' thing I've talked about.

Black and white version?

A man I couldn't stand came to teach me things about my life that before this time I had been very precious about. For example:

Don't anyone tell me ever how to bring up my kids or Daniel;

Don't anyone try and push me to look at my vulnerability – I'm doing fine;

Don't anyone tell me I'm giving too much and being a martyr;

Don't anyone tell me I spend too much time alone;

Don't anyone tell me I run when someone gets really close to my heart;

Don't anyone tell me I can't receive back;

Don't anyone dare tell me I don't know how to love or am afraid to get too intimate in case I lose control.

Okay that's just the tip of the iceberg of what Ian has challenged in me over this past year.

You've probably gathered from the book this far that in man's world, I know myself pretty well. I work hard on my love and compassion and on my Soul journey; I provide a loving, safe place for people to go through enormous amounts of stuff to find a deeper place inside themselves. All that is easy for me.

This place I was being challenged at was something much deeper and more vulnerable than I'd ever been game to look at. Yet it came wrapped in lessons that were clear, unmistakable and very simple.

One night I asked before I went to bed to be taken to where he was for once so that I could gain a different perspective. I found myself walking into a place he was working and there he was actually on the computer screen. He looked out at me with blank eyes and I thought, 'Good that's that then' and started to head out of the door. I saw another guy I knew from the same place and he was tied up in ropes. I asked if he wanted me to untie him but he said "No" – he needed to be tied up. I wanted to help him but he looked very forlorn and said "No". As I was leaving again I saw a woman I knew there and she started yelling at me that I had not supported her.

This clearly wasn't going well so I started to head for home. As I left I heard Ian's voice calling me loud and clear. I went looking for him and found him down at the end of an alleyway. He put his arms around me just for a moment, I felt that same strong place inside me and I left.

That's what happened in every dream for the first six months, Barely any words, I would be in situations where I was being extremely challenged in my work and he would be there, He would hold me for a moment or just stand and hold my hand and then I'd take on the challenge with more strength than I'd ever known.

Some colleagues and I had driven down the Great Ocean Road in Victoria to check out venues. It's actually where the energy to complete this book came in. We were sitting on top of a beautiful hill in Apollo Bay, watching the first light come up over the ocean. The photograph we took as that sun came up is on the cover of this book. We were discussing a few team members who apparently pull on me way too much and when I'm in work mode I miss the point where I start to get drained.

Here we were, miles from anywhere, minding our own business when Ian's voice came into my head with that forceful energy and said "That wouldn't happen if I was around".

Picture this now. I'm sitting on the top of a hill at dawn arguing with someone who wasn't even there.

I thanked God that morning for that small mercy – that Ian wasn't there and wasn't likely to be – because I'm positive we would come to blows in mans' world in no time at all.

Now I have to be honest and own the fact that a few days later, it slowly started to dawn on me that he was right. At first, those times were very bitter pills for my ego to swallow let me tell you, though of course somewhere my heart knew the truth.

You wouldn't believe how many nights I woke up and tantrumed up and down the front deck at 3.00 am pleading to have an answer as to why it would have to be him that helped me. I didn't need anyone.

I realised I had never needed anyone emotionally like that before in my life. I remember coming home one night after work when I was first living with Arch, and a young girl I'd been working with had committed suicide. She was thirteen and when I told Arch what had happened he wanted me to talk and tell him about how I was feeling.

This was really weird for me, I looked at him with what must have been a really strange look. Like 'What do you mean, I don't need to share this. I'm fine'. All about me of course, but I had no idea how to share that part of myself with anyone.

At Jo's funeral, I had all the kids sorted, I was

keeping an eye on everyone, making sure Mum and Nanna had someone holding them up – literally. Sure I was crying pretty hard a lot of the time but I did not want one person to come and comfort me or do anything about my emotional state. I was doing that myself thanks very much.

I remember looking down into the grave as the coffin went down, holding a child up on either side and for a second my legs went weak and I felt like I was going to fall. A second. Just one. Then I stood up and reprimanded myself for my weakness, I needed to be there for everyone else.

It didn't ever occur to me to say, "Could someone just hold me for a minute until I gather my strength?" Or, God forbid, that I might need someone to hold me so I could cry. That concept was, until a year ago, so far from my reality it was impossible to fathom in my rational mind.

I hold so many people in so many situations in workshops and in the world so they can feel stronger and allow themselves to cry and release their emotions. I am understanding this learning more and more each day. I cry a lot more than I ever have. Haven't actually got to the asking someone to hold me while I cry yet…. a work in progress maybe!

My friend Pete once told me he considered me to

be a good friend. We travelled and worked together, at times often for a week at a time. It was easy being with Pete. We enjoyed each other's company, there wasn't any fuss. We didn't have to entertain each other at any stage; we could just do our own thing.

He also said he could get so close and then that wall came up and that was it. No closer. As I'm writing this today I am beginning, just beginning to understand things a little more clearly.

This 'not needing anyone' is not a good thing. It's arrogant and dismissive. So I can love everyone and work with them and be there for them and hold them just as long as they don't want to do the same for me. As long as no one tries to give back to me emotionally.

I woke from a dream of Ian one morning in the surest, clearest most peaceful space I had ever been in. I sabotaged that feeling fairly quickly with my head running all the anger about 'This is crap, he's not even here and I don't want these stupid lessons one more day'. I ran off shopping and ended up a complete mess, crying, panicking and fearful that I was about to have some sort of major health crisis whilst driving my car. I drove down a beautiful road that I drive along often – the road where my grandfather worked in the flower farm while he was alive. I was throwing up down the front of my shirt and begging God for help. John said,

"You know who you need help from". I knew he meant Ian. I also knew he didn't mean call him physically.

I had myself in a state I couldn't get out of, which in itself is so out of character for me. I kept saying "Pull yourself together, you do not need anyone for anything". In the end I absolutely had to surrender or crash into a tree.

I called to Ian with everything that I am. "Please help me Ian. I'm afraid and I don't know what's happening to me". His voice echoed around my car, "I'm here, I don't know what to do, but I'm here".

The panic left in a second and that peaceful safe feeling returned and I drove home to clean myself up knowing I needed to change that part of me that doesn't admit to needing anything other than physical things from people. I needed support in that moment and I had to ask for it.

 There are still places in all of us that inhibit us from going right down to the core of who we are. To the strongest place of reality and Love that cannot be taken away from us. So many people move forward in a lot of areas of their life but there remains one part that inhibits the full potential.

Each one of us has that deep Knowing that is beyond the words. Beyond the scenarios we create. Beyond the stories the world tells to stay comfortable. Beyond the fear of losing control of our lives or of those around us. This experience has given me an insight into how much we humans will fight to stay in that place we know and an insight into the gifts that are on the other side.

I am a strong capable woman. Under pressure I'm confident. Still, I had this part of me that did not want to receive anything from others. How on earth could I value people if I didn't receive anything back from them?

I am deeply honoured that I was given the opportunity to find this place inside me. My already passionate expansive life has taken on a whole new meaning.

This has been the greatest learning ever of being able to know what I know and hold that under all kinds of opposition. To get to a place of feeling something that no person or thing can pull me out of, or tell me is not real. To the place where I rarely second-guess myself now.

It's what I've fought for my whole life and it's slowly coming into reality for me.

To be given this experience and to have fought it

every inch of the way to the surrender. Then feeling that surrender and feeling it bring home to me the greatest strength I have and will ever know, is the very reason I find myself sitting on my front verandah at dawn, often sobbing with gratitude at the gift I have been given and the level of Love in my heart now for God, John, Nature, the Teacher and also for Ian. For myself, my friends and my clients from a place I had never known and would not have known without this experience. I can go now to that softer place that allows me to love wholeheartedly without any expectation or agendas.

I know without doubt that if I had not been given this opportunity and challenged daily as I have been, pushed into places I did not want to go, been told to go to the deep Love that's in my heart and feel the truth of that, then I would not have had the courage to push through the many obstacles that have stood in the way of writing this book. The many people who have given their 'helpful' comments about the book itself and my work. The couple of people I was brave enough to share the contents of this chapter and much more with after months of confusion, who 'lovingly' told me to get over myself, handing out lots of syrupy comments that effectively put the lid on my feelings for a time and left me feeling like a complete idiot.

Still in my gut the stirring was there. Still the dreams came six nights a week. Still my guidance was there clear as day telling me to hold the love in my heart for Ian.

I had to find a place of knowing me that was so sure and unshakeable even in this vulnerable area, so I couldn't be pulled off-track.

I have always believed being vulnerable is being weak. I have learned without any shadow of a doubt that being vulnerable is one of the strongest places I can work from.

I realised that whatever people thought about what was happening for me, they were not experiencing it. Only I knew what was happening and I needed to learn again that if these people took on board what I was saying and believed it was actually the truth, then they would have to look at that vulnerable part of their own lives. Perhaps their lives may need to change. Of course it made sense that they would be attempting to shut me down.

What I would have done in the past where intimacy is concerned was believe everything they said, and once again dismiss the journey I needed to undertake. Then this book would never have come to fruition and the learning would once again have been missed.

This time I had Ian's energy behind me, constantly pushing me into that vulnerable place where I needed to listen and understand that I could drop my resistance and my fear of needing someone, albeit energetically. His support was a strength I have learned to rely on to stand up time and time again against things I would definitely have wobbled about before.

Even the fact that Ian has no knowledge of this whatsoever is a huge challenge for me. A challenge to continue to hold the Knowing I have, and the clarity of my dreams and my intuition and just simply keep loving him for whatever reason I have to in order for me to keep moving into my Soul journey with everything that I am.

This was not the minds' attempt to make this into a 'wants' type of love – you know, the kind that yearns for someone and *wants* to be around them, to make contact with them or let the fantasies run away in your head with 'what-could-be's. This was what I was being told I *needed* to do.

Many many times over this period John would say to me, "You know what you know. Get out there and share it".

What I had to learn was to go past everything that my head had ever told me about this guy, everything I felt for so many years, to go past all of that and find such a strong, sure love inside my heart for him that my life and my work expanded to heights I could never imagine. Then I could step out from behind everyone I had put in front of me in my life and do what I'm meant to do.

To work a room full of people from a deeper loving connection than ever before and experience the joy of seeing these people transform, which has time and again in the past few months had me in tears. Which is not usual for me. I love my work and am always thrilled to see people move forward but this feeling in my heart now is hard to talk about in words.

I had to learn that while John was saying constantly, "Follow your heart" and my head was arguing that it wasn't possible, I had only to understand that I needed to listen to my heart.

I know that my greatest gift is the deep place of safety and trust I can hold now for myself and for others. The place of Knowing even when the head wants to tell me otherwise. Being able to get further under my own stories to trust now that what I know is what I know and to hold for that at all times.

I've learned again that our minds can so warp what is going on in our lives. We are at Step 27 before we can even feel what Step 1 is all about. I knew that concept but to be pushed again in this very sensitive area has been the most challenging and rewarding learning of all.

As I said at the beginning, this chapter is the culmination of all my learning. It's what I've learned to believe in.

Being made a fool of is something I struggled a lot with in my younger years. It hardly bothers me now, but laying my heart on the table like this and sharing things with strangers about my deepest fears and my deepest loving place is probably a reasonable time to feel a bit shaky about making a fool of myself.

Well this morning I'm leaving that fear behind as well.

This week has been a struggle as Dan desperately needs a birth certificate to obtain his passport to head overseas within three weeks. It was difficult to find Cheryl, and Dan has never had a birth certificate, so there has been lots going on. Meanwhile, I've been attempting to re-write this chapter and having to go to the bush often to stay on-track. I've been asking God, "What can I do to make this situation with Cheryl easier? We can't actually find her and time is running out for Dan and his passport". Each time I asked I was told "Hold your Love for Ian".

Yes, it's as weird as it comes, I know...

But over this time I've learned to trust this and

things open before me. As they did that very day five minutes after being told that, trusting it, going to that place and like a miracle having Cheryl on the phone. She stepped up and did what was needed with twenty four hours and I now have Dan's birth certificate in my hand and all passport info signed by his mum.

At first, nine months ago, I fought tooth and nail with this 'weird' guidance. I argued that I didn't even know this damn bloke and what I did know I didn't even like, let alone 'hold love for him'. In meetings where I was about to face some pretty tough opposition and the last thing on my mind was him, I'd ask what I needed to do and that's what I'd be told over and over again. I was told my heart needed a chance to love him. Not for him to love me, but for me to love him.

I didn't ever want to write these things in here. Well, bugger it, I'm writing it.

I fought this until about three months ago. Once I surrendered, life has opened up into helping and being helped like I have never known before.

Another thing. Cheryl passed on a message to me last night when she arrived from Violet, her mother, Daniel's nan, who had recently been diagnosed with tuberculosis. At present she is in hospital undergoing intense treatment to deal with her condition.

Cheryl gave her the manuscript of this book to read in hospital.

The message Violet sent was this:

"Please tell Helen that her book has inspired me to live. Not only to live but live a better and more full life than I've ever done before. It's the most inspiring thing I've ever read and I now have hope at sixty-five that I can have a better life if I'm willing to fight for it. I didn't know I could fight for it until I read this book. I thought all I could do was accept what was. Now I know differently and I am going home next week to fight for me and my life."

So that's what this is all about. This book, this chapter about Ian. Not about me personally having some thing going on with some guy. It is so far away from that. It's about me having enough humility to believe God even when my ego wanted to scream 'No this can't be, not this guy'. It's believing what I'm being asked to believe and actioning without questioning it or worrying about the outcome. It's about going to the deep Love in my heart, knowing it and then being brave enough to hold onto it.

It's about writing this book with clarity and real honesty no matter how I look to the outside world to give people like Violet the courage to stand up, grab their own brass ring and fight for their life.

For me these are the things that are worth look-ing like a fool for.

These are the things I will fight for until I drop.

35

The Nature Connection

FROM MY EARLIEST MEMORY WITH MY GRANDFATHER THROUGH to today, Nature has been a massive part of my learning and now my teaching.

No matter what was going on I could walk in the bush or swim in the ocean. Plant something in the garden or simply walk around and see what had grown that day. I sometimes sit for hours in the bush next to my home and just watch. I was instructed by John this year, just before my birthday, that if anyone asked what I wanted I was to ask for a good camera. This challenged me for a few reasons. Firstly, the only ones who would ask would be my kids, which they did every year, and I always said the same thing, "I don't need a present from you. Spend your money on something for yourself, or the kids". Besides I could never think of what I wanted. Or is it just that I like to buy things myself?

Anyhow I did what I was asked, and received a beautiful 'whizz-bang' digital job that you can load straight onto the laptop. Gorgeous really. I haven't figured a lot of it out yet and of course I haven't read the manual, but what I have worked out is how to take the most beautiful close-ups of everything I see. Flowers, animals, even weeds. Those things we madly rip out of our garden are so beautiful and precious and I have the photos to prove it. It's given me an even deeper respect and Love for Nature and all that entails.

I still weed the garden but I do it with a lot more respect these days. The team is setting about making a calendar for next year to show people what is out there and the detail involved in the creation of every single thing on this planet.

Nature always takes me to another place. My friend Kathryn and I have been known to dip into the icy ocean in Tasmania for an early morning swim in the middle of winter. Nothing better to clear the head than that, I can tell you!

I've spent a lot of time in the bush with my Aboriginal friends and learned many things about how gentle and nurturing and also how tough Nature can be. I learned to steep Australian bush flowers and use them for healing purposes. These people showed me how simple and effective these remedies can be and they're right under our noses.

We ignore so much of the beauty that surrounds us. I watch people who power-walk on the beach in the mornings when I visit the Sunshine Coast in Queensland. Hundreds of busy walkers, heads down, headphones on, going for it. Getting their bodies fit with their minds fully focused on the task. Meanwhile, there is the most astounding sunrise happening across the ocean just over their shoulder. All they have to do is turn their heads and feel the power of what's going on out there.

I spent some time in Victoria with an Aboriginal man some years back. We spent a lot of time just sitting on the water's edge fishing for our dinner, or amongst the towering gums where he lived. At the time a lot of the Aboriginal people were being moved from their bush homes into houses in a nearby suburb. This transition took them way out of their reality and they reacted accordingly.

What was true for this man was his connection with Nature, with the land that touched his heart. It fed him and it sustained him. He explained to me that when he was moved into the town he asked "Why?" and was told it was 'better for him'. Good grief! Anyway, he asked the people delivering the message how they would feel being out there where he lived, in the bush, with no shops or houses. Of course they didn't even consider his question. He was moved into town and spent some miserable years doing what he was told.

I asked him what he'd learned from that experience. He said to me: "White man knows what he sees, black man knows what he feels." That made a lot of sense to me.

There were times I would go to a river bank and sit for hours watching the water do its trip downstream. It was definitely my salvation a lot of the time, but I know I also hid there quite a bit. I felt safe and connected and didn't have to explain myself. These days I do a lot of talking to people about how they can connect back to the simple basics of life by starting with a single plant and then building.

My grandfather, in his later life, worked in a nursery. I would go with him sometimes, and watch him work with the plants he grew there. He truly loved them. He had enormous respect for Nature and I thank God I learned that from him.

That was one of the things I loved about Arch. His love of Nature and his knowledge of trees and plants and birds was extraordinary. I learned heaps from him. I remember one night we were heading out for dinner somewhere. I'd worked fifteen hours straight as I do, rushed in for a shower and then went to head out of the door. We were already late and it was a hot night. I looked everywhere for Arch and finally found him with the hose in his hand watering the garden.

I have to say, that day it was a gruff, "Come on, we've got to get there". But there was no way he was leaving until the plants had been watered. What he said to me was, "Can't you feel their distress?" When I stopped long enough I could. We watered the entire garden, missed the dinner and I felt blessed to witness someone able to take that kind of care.

If we take notice, Nature could be our greatest teacher. If we don't take notice it will teach us anyway. Natural disasters are happening more and more often. We ignore the small warnings. Our rivers are being polluted to the point of drying up and dying and trees are being cut down. I heard a woman say last week she was afraid of wind as the trees might fall on her. Her fear was palatable. Trees allow us the air that we breathe. Now people want to get rid of them in case they fall over.

We use chemicals on everything because it's easier. We buy conveniently, without thought, to make our lives easier. Without considering what it actually does to the future of our world.

Now Bird Flu has people in full panic mode. Millions of birds are being slain in China 'just in case'. This is obviously a problem but we are reacting out of fear. I don't watch TV, but I've been told the media are whipping up a frenzy and the fear in the world community is rife. I'm certainly not saying there is nothing to be concerned about. We could lose our lives from this dreaded disease but I'm not worrying about that in advance.

This is another strong example of people in their heads rather than in their Knowing. If the people in charge of this mania would stop their own heads and go to their Knowing, to the actual truth of what's going on it could be dealt with.

A while ago I was in Pambula in New South Wales for a week. It's a beautiful place with beautiful birds. Toby and I fed them every morning and they would hop down onto our breakfast bowls and chat away. Toby was delighted, it was a beautiful time. A woman in the next house who was just arriving for her holidays saw what was going on and yelled out to me that the bird flu was here and we needed to shoo the birds away. I laughed and told her I felt very safe with them and had many, many birds around my home and felt fine with it. She and her husband packed their car and left. They gave up their holiday for fear of catching bird flu.

 We're not being responsible occupants of our home. We are using earth's resources like bench-top appliances. We've done the maintenance checks but we're not actually doing the maintenance because appliances are replaceable – but earth's resources aren't.

Our mortality consciousness makes us believe that we have a right to get what we want now, take what we want now and use what we want now – because we can't take it with us. We seem to have forgotten that our children inherit the family home and that our great-grandchildren will also reside at the same address: Planet Earth. Nature does not need us to survive. We need it.

We have an opportunity to learn from Nature and we continue to try and control it. Are we not getting the message when things like the recent tsunami take place? Nature is warning us that we are taking far more than we are giving. If we don't turn this around we will suffer the consequences.

I recently heard a quote from a respected futurist that said: "In my opinion humanity has a fifty-fifty chance of surviving the next hundred years." Doesn't this make people sit up and take notice? Obviously not.

I received an email from someone I know, asking me to sign my name and help save the rainforests in Brazil. While I believe saving the rainforests in Brazil is a vital thing to do and am one hundred per cent behind anyone who is actively involved in doing that, I happened to be at this woman's home earlier that year and had seen her 'cave in' to some pressure from her neighbours to chop down a beautiful gum tree in her own back yard that had thrown a couple of branches. There was no fight in her whatsoever for her own environment. Of course safety has to be considered, but there was a way to create a win/win situation and not destroy the tree. How can you then send an email to save a rainforest? Of course you can, because then you don't actually have to put yourself on the line and do anything personally except hit the 'send' button.

This is just one of hundreds of stories I have of people being too lazy to step up and be responsible. It's easier to help something way outside of yourself that you never actually have to be responsible for. Makes you feel better. Does absolutely nothing for the planet.

John explained to me very succinctly that the responsibility begins with each and every one of us. It starts in our own homes, taking personal responsibility for our environment, our energy and the way we use it and how that impacts on others. He showed me a line of vibration that reaches across the planet through each home, through each family or individual. The negative talk, the anger and the unspoken words, the frustrations of not communicating our Love to each other and of competing with each other for energy, all add to the negative vibration that sets us up to be warned by Nature time and time again that we are not taking care.

My work is richly enhanced by my connection with Nature. As I've said, I rise at dawn each day and sit quietly in the bush as the natural world wakes up. It's a very special time for me and I know this gives me enormous amounts of energy to work with each day. It drops me to a place of being able to connect with my Knowing instead of my head. It's where I get to ask for the guidance from Nature to help me stay on track during my days.

In return, I work as often as possible in my garden. I am aware of and do my part in creating safe havens for the native birds. In my company we are involved in doing our part to take care of the local park and nature reserve. I teach as many people as will listen about the simple connections to Nature, and the give and take that can enhance lives as well as assist Nature.

However, I see so many people who are oblivious to the fact that Nature even exists really. Sure they know it's there but it's more as a convenience. A swim in the ocean, a walk in a park. It's all about them. All about them getting to see the beauty. Nothing about giving back or understanding that we need to actually connect and feel what needs to be done

36

Lessons from the Grandchildren

I COULDN'T POSSIBLY WRITE A BOOK AND NOT TALK ABOUT my connection with my four beautiful grandchildren. They are a light in my life that drives me out there to do the work I do in the world in the hope that they will understand who they are and truly feel their Place in the Boat.

As I've mentioned, my kids and their partners are wonderful, strong people. It stands to reason these kids are going to be strong individual little beings. And they are.

Toby was the first-born. He is five. Chelsea is four months younger and was born in March. Heath was born the day after I arrived home from that training at the beginning of May 2003 and Lucy was born twenty days later at the end of May. The timing of the pregnancies wasn't planned but the kids are very close in age and very close as cousins. Niki and Damian have the boys, Peta and Luke have the girls.

They are each beautiful, spontaneous and often outrageous and I love them dearly. We walk in the bush, we paint and make play doh. I've taught them how to make mosaic tables and pottery birdfeeders. We play in the rain and sit by the riverbank. Sometimes we get up at dawn together and lie on the grass in the dark watching the stars. We swim in the creek in winter and we make mud pies.

I had Chelsea, Lucy and Heath at my place last week and it was a little hectic. Heathy was doing his 'climbing to the top of the cupboard' thing and the girls were each doing a different activity. It was hot and sticky and I was obviously a little less patient than usual. I spoke to Chelsea about something she was doing, literally just spoke to her but my energy obviously displayed a little frustration. She looked up at me and said "I don't like it when you treat me like that, Nan".

A reaction started to rise up in me from being

told this by a four-year-old. After all, I didn't then, and never do, raise my voice to them. But I looked at her face and went to my energy to see how it was feeling and she was right. I never speak to them with frustration in my energy. I needed to get over myself.

Of course I give them boundaries to keep them safe while they're with me. But I don't beat them up energetically. I don't use manipulation with them. I don't bribe them or threaten them with things. We are clear with each other. We know what the boundaries are and we work within them to explore and discover and have fun. That's how it is while they're with me.

I also needed to learn to allow my children to be parents without any interference from me. I could do that, I've never really stuck my nose into my kids business but it wasn't always as easy as I thought. I've mentioned comments I've made, albeit slight ones, about them taking care of the kids. It's like the mother in me somehow thinks I know more because they are my children and now they have children.

It's been an unfolding for us, with me learning to step in when needed and step out when not needed. It was funny in the beginning when the little ones were babies to receive notes from my girls about how to take care of their kids. When to do what and how to do it etc. I learned to trust them and their own ways of bringing up their kids. It isn't always what I'd do but I completely respect their parenting.

Besides that, if I'm sticking my nose in too much it means I want some responsibility for the kids and I actually don't. It took me a while to get that. Of course I am responsible for them when I'm taking care of them, but other than that it's over to their parents and that is so freeing.

I've seen many clients who have grandchildren and are so involved in their lives that they fight with their kids about them. I actually want a life of my own and in the past year I've been saying "No" quite a few times to the baby-sitting stints.

It was hard for me to look at them and love them so much and absolutely love spending time with them but then separate out where I was going over the boundaries for myself. I would feel it instinctively when I'd had them for too long or too often. I'd feel a little guilty in the beginning about saying so but not now. They have wonderful capable parents. They each have another set of grandparents on their paternal sides who are a wonderful support to them as well. These kids are very loved and very taken care of. I'm happy to be the slightly left-field 'Nanny H' who does 'different' things with them. And then step out and live my own life. Works wonders.

Having said that it is a joy to watch them grow and develop and to connect them to Nature and themselves as much as I can possibly do in the time I spend with them. When any one of the four of them tell me "I love you, Nanny H", it never ceases to bring tears to my eyes.

A FOOTNOTE TO THIS CHAPTER:

17th January 2006 – Daniel called from work today. The conversation went like this:

"Nan?"

"Hi Dan."

"Are you home at four o'clock?"

"Yes".

"Got some people coming up to talk to you."

"Okay. Who?"

"Oh, some people from footy. We're going on a trip."

"Oh, great Dan! Where to?"

"South Africa."

"WHAT?!!!"

"Nan?"

"Yeah Dan?"

"Can you bring my phone down to work, please?"

The facts here are that Daniel has been chosen as one of two indigenous boys from Victoria and one of twenty from around Australia who will travel to South Africa next month to tour the country for two and a half weeks, play football against South Africa and run football clinics for young children. The tour has been organized by Qantas Airlines and the Australian Football League (AFL). As Mark Heaney said, "The hits just keep on coming for this boy".

Five minutes later the phone rings again. It's Lucy, my two-year-old granddaughter:

"Nan?"
"Yeah baby?"
"I JUST DID POO ON THE TOILET ALL BY MYSELF."

The 17th of January 2006 turned out to be an auspicious day in our household all round.

37

Shit Happens

THROUGHOUT MY LIFE THE CHALLENGES THAT HAVE COME HAVE served me well. If I'd never been confronted with these things, I know in my heart I would not be the passionate person I am right now. We all have different journeys and this is mine. I chose it and I've done my best to learn from what has been given to me so far.

I see people who lie awake worrying about things. Things that may never happen. Stuff going around in their heads about things they cannot now nor will ever be able to control. It's a serious waste of energy.

The fear in our society cripples us. Christopher Reeves said: "For able-bodied people paralysis is a choice. And it's not an acceptable one."

There are lots of things said about victims. There were many examples in my life when I could have chosen to be a victim to my circumstances and at times I probably made that choice. Once I learned I didn't have to be there I fought against it every time.

We are responsible for our own lives. Every single bit of them. Every single time we put one ounce of blame on someone else we are a victim to our circumstances. From illness to depression to tragedy – anything at all. We are responsible. We have to take full personal responsibility in every interaction that takes place. Every one without exception.

Even the Smiling Assassin is running his or her own energy underground to stay comfortable and to keep themselves from being exposed. Underground energy is a huge subject that we need to look at in this world – how we impact on each other with our energy and get away with it because all we see is what happens before our eyes. It's why John kept telling me,

"It's not about what you see, it's about what you know." There is a vast difference between the two.

I sit listening to people in my counselling room often and hear their 'stories'. In the first five minutes people normally tell me the truth of why they've come. It could be wrapped up in a whole lot of words but the truth will be there if you can track the energy of it. The 'story' is just what keeps that person safe. The *truth* is in the energy and often when I point out that I'm hearing a story and the actual energy is around *"so and so"* I get fierce resistance from the client because they are about to be exposed.

I have become skilled at exposing people honestly and with compassion so it makes the pill easier to swallow. The fact is if people take it on it's normally only a short time before they can belly laugh about how crazy it was and how freeing it is to recognize the fraud inside each one of us.

A clear example of this was one of my team members whose story had kept him stuck for forty years. This may sound ridiculous but I imagine everyone has a similar story that they tell to stay where they are.

Jeff told a story of being seven-years-old when out of the blue his parents told the two brothers they would be moving to an island. They'd be leaving their school and friends and it wasn't clear how long they'd be gone.

Fairly quickly this whole thing happened and Jeff was thrown into a new environment with no friends and he told how that still affects his life today and his relationship with his parents had been affected because of this lack of trust he felt for all people now.

I watched the room as he told the tale of woe and had everyone with tears in their eyes for this poor guy who had been marred so badly as a child. All I could feel was his energy. The story that came out of his mouth did not match the energy he was presenting. I said to him, "It feels like you had a great time on this island though." He looked at me briefly and said "Oh yeah, but..."

I laughed so hard I almost fell off the chair. He'd been 'sprung' and there was nowhere he could go. He laughed hard himself when he realised how long he'd kept that story going and the mileage he had got out of it over the years. The attention and energy he'd pulled to himself with that one 'story'.

When Duck first started with me several years ago, I was doing some work with her on the phone and she was telling me a great story about her life and how connected she was and about lots of esoteric fantasies that sounded to me like they were actually ruining her life and not enhancing it. All I could feel was that she was hiding. So of course I said that and she sheepishly replied that actually she had her parents staying with her from England and as she didn't have much space she was hiding in the wardrobe talking to me on the phone.

Pretty hilarious really. It turned out Duck was hiding in lots of other areas of her life as well. A footnote to that is the reason I call her Duck. Her name is actually Nicola 'Smith' let's say. Apparently that wasn't profound enough for her so she changed her name by deed poll to Nicola Falkan. After the beautiful falcon that flies so high above the world looking down on all us little plebs. Get the picture? Hence I call her Duck.

Thank God Duck can laugh about all this herself now and realizes how caught up she had been in being something else rather than finding out what made her tick and going for that. For all the supposed love and light she professed to have she was one of the loneliest people I'd ever met. Lonely with lots of lonely friends.

What I see so much of is people living life in fantasy so they don't have to step up and walk in their own life fully. That way, they don't have to take responsibility for what they create.

It's like the people who get hooked into movies and TV shows and then live their lives through that somehow. Movies like Lord of the Rings, and the Star Wars series. I'm sure they are brilliant movies and well-written. But then people rally behind the fight for some goblins and space characters who portray this battle between light and dark, while in their own day-to-day lives they have no fight. Mostly what I see is that they don't really know what's real or what they could be fighting for.

So what they do then is pick a battle that's not theirs. It's outside of them and easy to walk away from when they choose. How easy is it to watch a movie and get inspired and involved in these epic battles, but outside that cinema nothing changes? Or else to take the other easy option and get involved in someone else's battles: friends, neighbours, work colleagues, even world events. Or to allow others to get involved in your battles which only serves to pull you off-track.

It's still not owning that part in you that somewhere deep down knows what you need to fight for.

The fact is people *do* get inspired by the battles and want to shake their swords and take on the world, but in these movies the thing that's being fought for is clear up-front. In our own lives we have to find the truth of what the battles are *for us* and then fight from inside ourselves, usually with much opposition from the outside world. When you finally get to fight for what you know is the truth for you, the interesting thing to feel is that the battle subsides. You clearly stand up and hold that place but there is no raging battle anymore. It's such a strong sure place that the opposition of the entire world would not rock you.

So it's ironic that when we think the battle is about to begin, it's a battle of a whole other kind. Just the battle to know yourself and believe in that one hundred per cent. It's the battle to find and live from that place I speak of so often inside each one of us that is the hardest place to find and hold. But once there, *nothing* can shake you from that place.

From what I see the world is in a critical place. The choice is clear. Either we keep going the way we are right now, with the ego and the mind and all its' control running the show. Blaming people like George Bush and Osama Bin Laden for all the world tragedies and everything else in our lives that isn't going well. Or we can stand up, *right now.* And not from that wafty esoteric place that has us praying for peace and saving trees in Brazil. Praying is a great thing and I'm all for it, but if it's the only thing you're doing, and you are not working on your *own* energy and looking at how you impact on the world around you, then who is it helping?. The choice is to stand up from that place of taking total responsibility for 'you'.

For each and every one of you in your own homes, in your own environments. With every judgement you hold. Each time you look at another with underground energy running that is full of resentment or fear, in fact each time you control another person for any reason at all. Each time you control another from the place of 'helping them out' or doing it out of 'love', you are adding to the massive control energy that is destroying our planet. You yourself are adding to the 'warmonger mentality'.

Each time you pray for the 'less fortunate', I believe you are holding a judgment that their own Soul does not understand at some deep level what it is here to do. What if the 'less fortunate' have actually chosen their journey? Of course, that doesn't mean that there aren't people who are here to help out where they can, and the ones who are doing that are mostly doing a fabulous job, but if there is a judgment being held that the people who aren't like us *need* us to control their lives, I for one don't believe they do.

Imagine the sense of possibility that would be created from each person working on their own environment, on their own energy and how it impacts on others and *taking responsibility for that*. Creating real relationships that will enhance communities just by their very existence. Imagine the ripple effect of that around the globe...

The world dilemma is right in our faces. The horror of our news reports, the tragedies that take place every hour, the plight of our struggling planet all seem so overwhelming for most of us that we sit and watch it on TV, then we go to the movies to feel the fight and the passion for life. Then go home and watch the news again because we have absolutely no idea or conception of how to fight against the horror of the world.

The kids are fighting on computers because they don't know any other way.

What if we could make a planetary difference *every day* in our own small lives, in our own small way by having the courage to stand up and be responsible for what we ourselves are creating in every minute of our lives?

What if each one of us followed Violet Hayes and said "I am going home to fight for me and for my life"?

Not every one of us has to go and knock on George Bush's door with our opinions, or take a sword to whoever we perceive as the 'bad guys'.

It's time to stand up in our own energy and be counted. Each and every one of us.

What if then the ripple effect of our actions assisted our families and our communities and outwards?

If we don't start with us we will never start. Have the courage. Don't wait until your deathbed.

Do it now.

38

Coming Home to Me

PEOPLE ASK ME WHAT THEIR JOURNEY COULD BE. THEIR LIFE purpose. That 'what do I want to be when I grow up?' thing.

I tell them all it is for me is having the courage to find out who I am. And to learn to Love from that place with as much passion as I can at the time. To fight off the Wolves when they come. To be willing to take on new feelings and ideas that may be way out-side the realm of my thinking.

It isn't about being something. It isn't about proving something.

It is about being me and that is enough. Enough.

It is about being the best I can be in every moment with the wisdom I have gained so far. If I wait until I get it perfect I will never be able to fly. And I want to fly.

Once I made the decision to 'Live Until I Die' the doors opened everywhere.

We do an exercise in our workshops where people write their own eulogy. I believe some of the things people want to hear at their funeral are a reflection of how society is living the half-life. 'Trying' to get it right and be seen to be a good person.

When I die I want my eulogy to be:

"I had a crack at everything that came along. I was far from perfect but I reached for that brass ring with all of my heart. I gave to others from a real and clean place with no agendas. I loved and lived with all the passion I could muster."

Through the pages of this book my hope is that I've conveyed the journey from my head to my heart with enough clarity for even one person who reads it to pick up the ball and run with it and Live until You Die.

About MURAGAI Life Strategies

MURAGAI LIFE STRATEGIES (MLS) is the company established by Helen Daniel to deliver a new and revolutionary approach to life. Through its' series of seminars, programmes and teleconference calls, MLS assists people to take the message contained in this book and apply it directly to their own lives.

MLS programmes include a two-day interactive Live Until You Die event run personally by Helen Daniel in spectacular locations around Australia complete with stunning audio-visual presentations.

Full details, together with information on MLS' other programmes can be found on the MLS website, where there is also an opportunity to subscribe to its newsletter service and keep up-to-date with words 'from Helen's Desk'.

www.muragai.com

- It's for those who are tired of talk and need to act.
- It's for those of us who choose to fight for our Souls and for our planet and who choose to take personal responsibility for what we are creating.

Underpinning all of MLS's work is a strong connection to Nature and the land that is our home.

ISBN 141208284-6